# THE NEW JUSTICE
# FOR CHILDREN AND FAMILIES

and

# THE STORY OF CAMP OAKLAND, Inc.

Arthur E. Moore

*Library of Congress Catalog Card Number: 65-27423.*

*Published through the kind assistance of the*
AARON MENDELSON MEMORIAL TRUST.
*Gladys Dart, Surviving Trustee*
**AND**
*Harry Winston, Deceased Trustee*

# ABOUT THE AUTHOR

The author, Honorable Arthur E. Moore, now Circuit Judge, was Judge of the Juvenile Court of Oakland County, part of metropolitan Detroit, Michigan, for twenty four years. Some five thousand children and youth received his personal attention as court wards. Programs described in this book, including those of Camp Oakland, Inc., were instigated by Judge Moore and are effectively operating in Oakland County. Second in size in Michigan, Oakland County has a million people of families of every type and station in life.

Being a lawyer, Judge Moore has insisted that Juvenile Courts protect the most important American constitutional privilege, the right and privilege of children to enjoy discipline, affection and training in a secure, moral and religious home.

Deeply interested and experienced in social problems, he insists that the Juvenile Court has parental duties, that it must strengthen family ties by protective treatment and must afford training and education, saying—

"Courts must do more for children than the surgery of judgements, decrees and mandates. They must step down from the bench to the small hand of the child and the turned shoulder of the parent and find a new start for parent-child relationship".

Judge Moore urges that even partial solutions to family problems may avoid tragedy and degradation. He believes that justice to families requires both judicial and social action. He is deeply interested in the problems of children and their families and is eminently qualified to write concerning these problems and their solutions.

CARL O. BARTON, *President*
Camp Oakland, Inc.

4

HON. ARTHUR E. MOORE
*Circuit Judge and former Judge Juvenile and Probate Courts,*
*Oakland County, Michigan*
*Chairman Board of Directors Camp Oakland, Inc.*

5

*This book is dedicated to Ruth Gehrke and Ann and James Aliber, the family of the late Walter Gehrke, and to his multitude of friends in grateful appreciation of his everlasting services to children at Camp Oakland.*

WALTER GEHRKE, *Deceased*
*Former President Camp Oakland, Inc.*

7

# Table of Contents

|  | *Page* |
| --- | --- |
| Preface | 12 |
| Camp Oakland, Inc. and New Justice for Children | |
| Foreword | 16 |
| The New Justice for Children at Camp Oakland | |

## Part I

### History and Programs of Camp Oakland

| | |
| --- | --- |
| Chapter 1 | 18 |
| History of Camp Oakland Five Programs which Furnish Underprivileged Children "New Justice" | |
| Chapter II | 19 |
| First, There was Bill Norton | |
| Chapter III | 20 |
| Next, There was Jim Hunt | |
| Chapter IV | 23 |
| Walter Gehrke and Friends | |
| Chapter V | 26 |
| Locating Camp Oakland—Boys' Ranch | |
| Chapter VI | 31 |
| "Summer Camp" | |
| Chapter VII | 34 |
| Girls' Ranch | |
| Chapter VIII | 36 |
| Work-Education Camp | |
| Chapter IX | 40 |
| Family Camp Clinic | |
| Chapter X | 42 |
| Judge Stanton Dondero, Charles DeVlieg and the Dr. Blains | |
| Chapter XI | 45 |
| Bill Matus, Our Permanent Director and Leader in Youth Work at Camp Oakland | |

# Table of Contents

|  | *Page* |
| --- | --- |
| Chapter XII | 46 |
| The Oakland County Board of Supervisors | |

## PART II

### The Juvenile Court and New Justice

| | |
| --- | --- |
| Chapter XIII | 49 |
| Leadership in Prevention | |
| Chapter XIV | 51 |
| Prevention Must Precede Crime else it is Justice Sought Too Late | |
| Chapter XV | 55 |
| The Modern Juvenile Court | |
| Chapter XVI | 56 |
| The New Juvenile Court Provides New Justice for Children | |
| Vhapter XVII | 60 |
| Total Community Cooperation is New Justice | |
| Chapter XVIII | 63 |
| Children's Village—A Diagnostic Service Center for Needy Children and Youth | |

## PART III

### Protective Services and The Community

| | |
| --- | --- |
| Chapter XIX | 64 |
| Protective Services—Prevention of Delinquency | |
| Chapter XX | 67 |
| Emotional, and Other Neglect | |
| Chapter XXI | 70 |
| Delinquency is Inherited | |
| Chapter XXII | 71 |
| Characteristics of Delinquents | |
| Chapter XXIII | 74 |
| Prevention by Protection—The Great Objective | |

# Table of Contents

| | *Page* |
|---|---|
| Chapter XXIV | 76 |
| Delinquent Heritage | |
| Chapter XXV | 78 |
| Reaching Predelinquency | |
| Chapter XXVI | 80 |
| The Deficient Child Deserves "New Justice" | |
| Chapter XXVII | 86 |
| Prevention by Police—Aids New Justice | |
| Chapter XXVIII | 87 |
| Church Responsibility for New Justice | |
| Chapter XXIX | 88 |
| Religious Assistance is Protective Justice | |
| Chapter XXX | 91 |
| Divorce and the Broken Home—Justice Defeated | |

## PART IV

### Criminal Justice Needs Civil Procedures and Social Services

| | |
|---|---|
| Chapter XXXI | 95 |
| Present Criminal Procedure | |
| Chapter XXXII | 97 |
| New, Modern Justice Demands Social-Legal Progress | |
| Chapter XXXII | 99 |
| Our "One Court of Justice"—Needs Services | |
| Chapter XXXIV | 101 |
| Judicial Efficiency Demands Administrative Services | |
| Chapter XXXV | 103 |
| Our Criminal Procedure Needs Revision | |
| Board of Directors and Officers of Camp Oakland, Inc. | 111 |

CARL BARTON
*President Camp Oakland, Inc.*

11

# CAMP OAKLAND, INC.
## *and new justice for children*

This is the story of "New Justice for Children and Families" of America. The story of Camp Oakland is a vital part. Camp Oakland, Inc. is the finest organization for underprivileged children and youth in the United States.

Here in Oakland County, Michigan we have proved that judges and government on the one hand, and private citizenry—service clubs, churches and communities on the other—can all cooperatively serve children—and prevent neglect, delinquency and crime. This cooperative, community-wide service is the basis for New Justice for our underprivileged children.

So we tell the story of hundreds of people, many of whose names you will recognize, participating in New Justice for Children and in the work of Camp Oakland, Inc. Thousands more gave great assistance. But space does not permit mentioning them all.

Twelve years ago our citizens of Oakland County established several splendid programs for needy children and youth at Camp Oakland, Inc., at Oxford, Michigan. The simple purpose—to help children of the court and also children and families who might otherwise come before the Juvenile Court readjust into good citizenship.

*What is Camp Oakland, Inc?*

Camp Oakland, Inc. is a charitable, non-profit corporation which came into being simply because citizens of Oakland County, Michigan decided to solve the problems of delinquency and neglect.

There were children involved in their own communities. They decided to help these underprivileged children who had no adequate home, or were subject to improper home conditions. So to the boy or girl who deserves a home—the child who needs guidance, training and affection, the lad who wants to camp, swim and develop character:— "Boys' Ranch", "Girls' Ranch", "Family Clinic Camp", "Work Education Camp" and "Summer Camp", these programs at Camp Oakland, Inc. all offer personal care, correction and success in living; for hundreds of boys and girls in need of such assistance.

12

These five programs at Camp Oakland, Inc. are all an integral, important part of our 'New Justice for Children".

## Who are the Underprivileged Children of America?

In order to tell the story of New Justice for underprivileged boys and girls of America, this book describes the neglect and delinquency problem. It tells of the helpful community, the team service of the Juvenile Court and staff, and the need of improved child and family care, the work of Camp Oakland and the prevention of delinquency. This in total, is the "New Justice for Children." Camp Oakland is the vital center of child assistance.

## The Cause of Delinquency.

The root of all delinquency and child maladjustment is the lack of reasonable family care by ordinary good parents. Broken homes, divorced parents, inadequate custodians are the cause. The best institution, clinic, or guardian-custodian, cannot give children the security, affection, disciplinary training and encouragement every youngster so greatly needs from parents.

The real poverty of today is the deprivation of these improverished children. Homeless indeed!

Food, clothing and economic needs are minor deficiencies compared to lack of loving care and parental discipline.

Camp Oakland, Inc., a Michigan charitable corporation, operates its various programs as a substitute parent. By charter it is designed to assist underprivileged children, youth and families. To that end it is completely dedicated.

America will produce better families, happier children, more reliant youth—if we pursue the new concept of Justice for children described herein.

The Juvenile Court must have administrative arms. It is a team of Judge and staff of skilled specialists, working cooperately together; they must all have minds of child understanding and hearts of forgiveness. It must have facilities for warm shelter, careful diagnosis, kindly treatment, special education and affectionate guidance. Thus every case worker, probation officer, psychologist, counsellor, psychiatrist, cook and housemother is a component part of the court. Each plays an important part in the assistance program to aid the child.

Punitive treatment is a vice of the past. Punishment now arises only through our failure to help parents and children to understand; only when our human skills are inadequate to lighten their burdens, are children still so penalized.

The heart of delinquency prevention is the Samaritan assistance of each community towards its own families and children, long before delinquency, neglect and crime are engendered.

The roots of child decency lie in good family living. Good communities produce good families.

America can prevent delinquency and neglect. Crime rates may easily be cut in half. An upsurge of religious and moral training and strengthening of families and homelife will eliminate most of delinquency and crime. On this premise, here in Oakland County, Michigan, our "Protective Services" to children and families have reduced Juvenile Court delinquency volume by 50 percent.

This New Justice for children will reduce delinquency everywhere in America, if we really care!

ARTHUR E. MOORE,
*Chairman of the Board of*
*Camp Oakland, Inc.*

*At Camp Oakland: Nothing is more fun for youngsters than a horse, a donkey or other animals*

# CHAPTER II

# FIRST, THERE WAS BILL NORTON

To understand Camp Oakland, Inc. and "New Justice" one must understand the background.

More than 5 years before Camp Oakland began, William J. Norton, Executive Director of the Cousins Fund ("Children's Fund of Michigan"), aided the Oakland County Juvenile Court program. The Cousins Fund and its trustees gave us financial assistance. We began to board delinquent children in Boarding Homes—on farms, with people who liked children, rather than sending them to Correctional Schools and Reformatories.

Arnold Nique, then County Agent of Oakland County, was assigned the task of finding and supervising these boarding homes. He did a wonderful job and found many homes for delinquent youngsters. They did not need maximum security. They did need warm affection, discipline, and encouragement. These were youngsters who had violated the law. But they were children who had lost much of their self respect, who thought that no one really cared about them, and actually didn't know how to behave better. It was a most successful program.

Through this effort we, the Juvenile Court Judge and staff, taught ourselves. That there really is no great difference between delinquent and neglected children. Except as to the manner in which they acted out or exhibited their unhappiness and their maladjustment. So it must be said that the influence of William J. Norton was the beginning of our understanding. The beginning of our Protection of Children. The beginning of our community-wide care for children. The Modern Juvenile Court movement.

So, we now overlook the terminology involved and try to understand the individual child. Thus it was in these years we began to look through symptoms and see the inherent character of the child in trouble. To determine whether his trouble is within himself or arising from his parents or from society. Thus it was through the help of our psychological and psychiatric services that we began to learn much more about our children in deep trouble.

Interestingly enough, some years later, when we were just beginning Camp Oakland—out of a clear sky came a substantial personal check from William J. Norton to Camp Oakland. Just at the time when Walter Gehrke and I were having our greatest difficulties in raising funds for Camp Oakland. What an encouragement of confidence!

# CHAPTER III

# NEXT, THERE WAS JIM HUNT

James Hunt has become the most successful and efficient "Director of Children's Services" Michigan has ever known. We are very proud of his many accomplishments.

Sometime prior to 1953 James Hunt had the responsibility of all children who were wards of the Juvenile Court. So it was that Jim actually became the originator of Camp Oakland. It came about this way: As the war was in its worst stages, children who resided in our Juvenile Court institutions said to Mr. Hunt, "Why can't we go to Summer Camp like all of the other youngsters do who are not in trouble?" "Why are we treated differently?" "Why can't we have this opportunity?" So, though automobile tires and gasoline were scarce, Jim Hunt and a very fine assistant, Harold Cole of Holly, decided they would indeed take these delinquent and neglected youngsters on a summer camping expedition.

With four old cars they set out to take 18 boys to Drummond Island on a summer camp trip. A hard trip, but rewarding indeed in adventure, self-reliance and discipline. Most of all importance was this; here a boy had opportunity not only for camping but to be and live with men who really cared about him.

So successful was this camping trip that the youngsters insisted that it become a permanent project. So, for three years similar summer camp trips were had each summer the same hard way, in this most difficult manner.

JAMES HUNT
*Director Childrens' Services,*
*Oakland County and Juvenile Court*

*Our Boys of Boys Ranch, of whom we are very proud*

CHAPTER IV

# WALTER GEHRKE
## and Friends

The late Walter Gehrke was the great successful leader of Camp Oakland. It succeeded because of his genius, devotion and tremendous personal service.

Just at the time when James Hunt needed help the most to make his Summer Camping program possible, the Women's Society of Christ Church Cranbrook, became interested and came to the rescue. They were the ladies who raised the first Camp Oakland funds. They encouraged all of us to decide that we would have a permanent camp in Oakland County for underprivileged children. So, we began to plan for a permanent camp. We drew upon our friends and acquaintances who believed in children. Out of their efforts came our newly incorporated charitable corporation, then and now known as "Camp Oakland, Inc."

The late Sally St. Clair, our first president, as well as Mary Proctor and Madeline Shenefeld spent endless time assisting the Camp Oakland projects get under way.

It was my good friend Arthur Bassett, then Vice-President of the Detroit Trust Company, and one of our most helpful supporters, and president Sally St. Clair who said to me one day, "We suggest that Walter Gehrke, who is President of First Federal Savings of Detroit, be made the President of Camp Oakland." "He is deeply interested in children, though some do not know this, and would make a most excellent leader of the new Camp." And to our great pleasure, Walter Gehrke accepted.

So for these many years he was the President and the most active leader of Camp Oakland. He was both my best friend and in my judgment one of the greatest of men. His ability and intelligence were unsurpassed. May I hypothetically say that what America needs most of all these days is more great business leaders like Walter Gehrke. Men who will take time out of their busy and successful lives to be leaders in the welfare of young people and thus, in our nation as a whole.

So, here we were with our Camp Oakland organization duly incorporated, many friends interested, but still very little money to use for our great hopes and plans.

Camp Oakland thrived on the friendship and assistance of many other supporters. These included Mr. and Mrs. James Aliber, Walter Anderson, W. T. Arlund, John W. Armstrong, Mr. and Mrs. W. B. Calhoun, Mr. and Mrs. Robert Chambers, William Corfield, Bruce Dodds, Fred Erb, Harold and Betty Fitzgerald, Ford Motor Co., General Motors Corp., Mr. and Mrs. Austin Harmon, Perry Holmes, John Houghton, Allen Gornick, Watson Brown, and the late Harry Winston.

Other staunch supporters were Larry Jerome, Clarence Kimball, Harry Klein, Harry Klingler, Mr. and Mrs. Samuel Lang, Ruth Lansing, Arthur Lawson, Aaron Mendelson Memorial Trust, I. W. (Ike) Robertson, Sally (Mrs. John P.) St. Clair, deceased, Fred Sanders, Fotis (Nick) Takis, Wayne Oakland Bank, Mr. and Mrs. Malcolm Welty and Youth Activities Fund. Also the Skillman Foundation, Edwin S. George Foundation, Renville Wheat and Daily Tribune Fund.

Our Vice-presidents, Bob Chambers and Bill Dearth have also served our projects and needs unceasingly. Mrs. Ben (Helen) Mills, our Vice President, has devoted tremendous energy to publicizing Camp Oakland through annual benefit programs. These were invaluable and brought us great support. Her women's committees have worked devotedly in many projects.

*Mrs. Ben D. (Helen) Mills, Jane Wyman, actress and Walter Gehrke, President at Camp Oakland Premiere "Bon Voyage" Benefit Party*

CHAPTER V

# LOCATING CAMP OAKLAND—BOYS' RANCH

Walter Gehrke and I spent many Saturdays trudging over the countryside throughout Oakland County attempting to locate the best site for Camp Oakland. This was fun for Walter because he loved to walk in the countryside. We became the greatest of friends. We both naturally enjoyed the planning and anticipation of the future of this Camp for boys and girls.

One day as we visited with two old friends, Roy Annett and his son Bruce Annett, realtors of Pontiac, they said to us:

"We have just the place for your Camp Oakland project."

"It is the old Lafer Farm on Drahner Road, near Oxford."

So it was that we visited this fine old farm homestead. It was a perfect site. There were 320 acres of beautiful farm property. 50 acres of lovely Lake Handsome; there was a stately old homestead which later became the Boys' Ranch home; adjacent to the home building was a large barn which housed milk cows. General farming was in operation.

It was very doubtful whether Walter Gehrke or I knew less about farming, but we both knew that this property was ideal in every respect for our projects. The Annetts turned in their entire real estate commission as their gift toward the purchase price. So our directors bought Camp Oakland on land contract for $118,000. We acquired not only the 320 acre farm, buildings and equipment, but also the Lafer family dog, and of necessity 30 milk cows and 2 prize bulls.

So, we were in business—we owned the real estate, we had a corporate Board of Directors, and all we needed now was about $85,000, some permanent support and ways and means of carrying out this project which we thought so ideal for boys in need. So it was, in a quiet way, that Walter Gehrke and I went to see many people whom

26

*First Boy's Ranch home and now the Administration and Clinic Building*

*New Boy's Ranch Building*

*Group of Boys at Ranch*

we knew. We explained the need for assistance to underprivilged children. Everyone gave aid.

Among the many initial liberal donors were: Howard McGregor and Mr. and Mrs. Alfred Wilson of Rochester; Harold Fitzgerald and Robert Critchfield of Pontiac, Walter Gehrke, Henry Wenger, Stanley Kresge and Harry Winston of Detroit, and Carl Barton of Birmingham, now our President.

We set about the problem of making the homestead building useable as a home for twenty active youngsters. This cost an additional $20,000. We bought and installed much new sleeping and living equipment, bunk beds for the youngsters, fire escapes, etc., and we were soon ready to take care of twenty boys, wards of the Oakland County Juvenile Court. We considered and treated them not as delinquents, but rather as boys who, though homeless, were as valuable as our own if only given opportunity. We believed the security of an adequate home would aid their growth as good citizens. This proved to be immeasurably true.

*Summer Camp for Protective Service Children*

# Chapter VI

## "SUMMER CAMP"

As I pointed out previously, the first purpose of Camp Oakland was to provide a summer camp experience for underprivileged youngsters. The first Summer Camp was conducted in the main house for one summer on Lake Handsome and we served only children from our Oakland County Juvenile Court. As this again was most successful, we were requested to give summer camping experience to many, many more youngsters of the County who were not court wards.

So it was that we called together the leaders of all of the Service Clubs of the County. These clubs ultimately reached about 100 in number. They included Civitan Club Pontiac, Friendly League, Hazel Park Lion's Club, Men's Club Presbyterian Church, Drayton Plains, Oxford Rotary, Pontiac Elks, Pontiac Kiwanis, Pontiac Women's Club, Rotary of Pontiac and Rotary of Royal Oak, Birmingham Lion's and Exchange Club, West Pontiac Kiwanis and Royal Oak and Ferndale Kiwanis Clubs. After discussion the problems, they agreed that we should give many, many more youngsters the summer camp experience. They further agreed that they would pitch in and help. First of all, they built for us six summer cabins; these cabins were constructed by such organizations as the Birmingham Lions Club, Royal Oak Kiwanis, West Pontiac Kiwanis, Ferndale Kiwanis, DeVlieg Association and others. Business and professional men like Clancy Blenman of Birmingham Lions worked many hours driving nails. One camp cabin was built all in one day by the DeVlieg Machine Company men. They brought along a registered nurse standing by ready to administer to the many banged fingers.

But we also needed a new assembly and dining building. So, we again went to our old friend, Stanley Kresge, and through his understanding and interest the Kresge Foundation gave us $15,000 toward a total of $30,000 which was raised and with which we built the main Summer Camp Building. So, at the end of the second summer we could and did take 100 boys at a time, 12 years of age and under, coming from all of the most underprivileged areas of the County, all

*Happy Kids at Summer Camp*

*Lunch Time, Kresge Bldg. Summer Camp*

referred by Social Agencies and Welfare Groups. Each boy or girl was given a 2 week's camping experience of his very own.

So 500 underprivileged children came to Camp Oakland each summer. Boys in the cabins on the east side of the main building and girls on the west. Some of them had never seen a fish before. They would walk along the lake shore looking at all the water life and catching frogs, fish and what not. Youngsters who had never been in swimming. Most learned to swim at camp. These boys and girls had the most delightful summer they had ever experienced, even as you or I. Many of the children tried to drink three quarts of milk the first day—for fear it would run out.

This then, was the beginning of Summer Camp Oakland. It was perhaps the most interesting of the five programs insofar as the general public appeal was concerned.

And to this day, this Summer Camp is sustained principally by the many various service clubs of the County. Clubs in numbers too great to mention. So, at this point, we had a year-round home for 20 boys, known as Boys' Ranch and we had a Summer Camp accommodating 100 youngsters at a time for five sessions of two weeks each, so that we had each summer 500 underprivileged boys and girls receiving the advantages of summer camp.

Soon the 500 children of Summer Camp, and the 100 parents and children of Family Camp Clinic were coming to us by referrals from all over the County by the respective Protective Service Committees. We have two requests for every camp membership available.

To raise our annual budgets for Summer Camp and Family Camp Clinic our committee chairman, Ike Robertson, set to work. For several years now he has called up his own Service Club, Birmingham High Twelve, to set the pace. One hundred other clubs and organizations also help. They have always given generously.

Our friends, Elmer Dieterle of Keego Harbor, Jim Sullivan of Royal Oak, and Manley Bailey of Birmingham, put on free dinner parties for the 100 Service Club presidents of the County. This with camp movies engendered much good will. Thus, the Service Clubs and similar organizations have kept Summer Camp and Family Camp Clinic operating each summer.

So it is that every community of the County sends us its underprivileged and every community's Service Clubs help underwrite the expense.

"As ye do unto others,"

"Ike" Robertson of Birmingham has headed the drive year after year with great success. Because everyone knows Ike loves these children.

*Girls' Ranch Building*

# CHAPTER VII

# GIRLS' RANCH

Soon there came to us many people who said, "You have done all these things for boys, why cannot girls have an equal opportunity?" And so it was that the Women's Service Clubs of this County, 34 in number, took upon themselves the joint venture to build what later became Girls' Ranch home building. Here again, these clubs were too numerous to mention and so many people participated that they cannot all be named. They set out to raise initially $20,000 and did actually raise a considerably larger sum of money.

With their help and by solicitation of others, and again by the aid of the Kresge Foundation, a fine Girls' Ranch building costing when equipped in excess of $100,000, was built upon the property. This fine building then enabled us to care for from 16 to 20 girls of all ages,

*Group of Girls at Girls' Ranch*

who needed a home, were underprivileged and had social problems which could not be handled in any other way. No finer home and program was ever provided anywhere than that for our youngsters at Girls' Ranch.

Kathryn Shields, Pearl Newcomb, Marguerite Newhouse, Helen Campbell and many other club leaders brought aid to the Girls' Ranch project by many women's service clubs and organizations. These included Altrusa Club, Birmingham Soroptimist, Birmingham Woman's Club, Business and Professional Women's Clubs, Ferndale Soroptimist, Quota Club, Soroptimist Club Royal Oak, Zonta Clubs of Ferndale and Royal Oak, and Zonta Club of Pontiac.

Sororities have aided our youngsters including Kappa Alpha Theta Alumni who undertook personal friendships programs with our girls.

*Work Education Group*

# CHAPTER VIII

# WORK-EDUCATION CAMP

Many court wards of 15 and 16 years of age are school drop-outs. They read at about the third grade level, are out of school, unemployable and have no interest in anything good. They are bound to get in trouble.

They are educationally and socially retarded but of normal mentality. These are America's wasted human resource.

So we first used our Summer Camp facilities to house these boys and provide for them a winter camp program. One combining learning to work with rapid up-grading of their reading. Being most successful, it is now a year 'round program. Special reading material to fit their low reading ability but older youth interest is provided, along with other accelerating, learning devices. They learn self pride, energetic working habits and to be useful.

Half of each day they are in the special school program. The other half of each day they spend at work assignments where they do useful labor. Everything of a work nature in and about the farm and the various Camp Oakland buildings. These include cutting and trimming

*Work Education at Study*

trees and brush, sawing wood, painting buildings and various unkeep and repair jobs.

We were fortunate in obtaining a splendid leader whom the boys like immensely, Gale Shafer. He works with the boys and also has installed an auto maintenance and simple auto repair shop. Every boy likes automobiles, so here is both a natural interest, a good trade, and a future livelihood as a good gas station attendant.

Our President Carl Barton has long given generously of his time, money and personal planning. Director Earl Green added many hours toward building plans.

So the boys, themselves, with Mr. Shafer's supervision, built a large living, eating and sleeping quarters accommodating 20 or more boys. This, added to the auto shop building, general work building and new rustic schoolroom have given us a real Work-Education Camp.

Boys appreciate the opportunity and so there are no runaways.

Work-Education Camp was operating successfully several years before our present national Poverty Programs. Poverty of delinquent neglected, maltrained or character deprived children ought to be restored to public interest. These are the real poverty stricken. Surely the poverty of abused and disadvantaged children—such child poverty is the root of all so-called poverty, however now exhibited or defined.

The Ford Fund and General Motors both have aided the project.

37

*Work-Education Camp Dormitory; constructed by the Boys themselves and their Supervisor, Gale Shafer*

*Work-Education Camp makes "Drop Outs" good citizens; of whom we are very proud*

CHAPTER IX

# FAMILY CAMP CLINIC

Soon we found that many families known to us needed family camping and skilled social services. This brought out the simple plan of giving the mother and her children camping fun. They would then trust us to help with their social and family plans.

As a result we set aside two weeks of camp facilities at Camp Oakland and invited, through our Protective Service units, mothers and their whole families. They averaged six children per family.

Our college counselors immediately took the children off the mothers' hands. The mothers were most grateful. Some had never experienced a single day free of the care of their children. Fathers were invited too, of course, but rarely showed up, though some were glad to come out and fish and have meals.

After the first day of relaxation and fun we offered the mothers two group counseling sessions per day to discuss and have assistance and learn about family problems. We found them eager for this assistance and trusting us, they opened up their problems and discussed them freely.

Sessions have varied at different years Family Camp Clinics. Sometimes the chief problem was alcoholism; sometimes adolescence, discipline, boy-girl relationship, sex behavior, failure in school, psychology of child behavior, personal health and cleanliness. Experts of all types were brought in to aid the discussions—psychiatrists, psychologists, teachers, public health nurses, A.A. leaders and youth counselors.

Letters of thanks and appreciation come from nearly all mothers after camp has terminated.

So successful has Summer Camp Clinic been that many of the Protective Service Committees of the various cities have set up similar counseling sessions for the winter time. Parents attended with the same attitudes and success.

So Summer Camp Clinic has continued from year to year aiding underprivileged families referred by the various local Protective Service Committees. The success formula is very simple—find the families in need; give them fun and friendship; having gained their confidence they are eager for skilled assistance whereby they can help themselves.

40

*Counselling at Family Camp Clinic*

CHAPTER X

# JUDGE STANTON DONDERO

# CHARLES DeVLIEG and the DR. BLAINS

One of those early days as I sat in my office wondering where $100,000 was going to come from to pay the balance needed to buy the Camp Oakland property, a good personal friend, Judge Stanton Dondero, then a practicing attorney in Royal Oak, came into my office and quietly said, "I understand you need money for your children's camp project?" Judge Dondero, thereupon obtained and made us a gift of $20,000 from a trust fund which he was administering. This then was the beginning of the raising of money beyond the concept of any of us at that particular time.

Perhaps this was the forerunner of later generosity. At all events, most unusual and generous gifts later came to us.

Charles DeVlieg recently gave Camp Oakland property of unusual value. And previously, Dr. Alexander Blain III and Dr. James Blain gave us most of Blain Island at Maceday Lake.

42

*Great fun on Camp Oakland's private lake*

*Youngsters are Well Behaved and Alert under Bill Matus' Affectionate Guidance at Camp Oakland*

# CHAPTER XI

# BILL MATUS, OUR PERMANENT DIRECTOR AND LEADER IN YOUTH WORK AT CAMP OAKLAND

On our staff of the Juvenile Court was a fine young man who wanted the opportunity of becoming Manager of Camp Oakland. So it was that William Matus took up his residency at Camp Oakland, first with the boys and later in the old farm house. From the beginning he has been truly a father to the boys assigned to Camp Oakland. He proved to be not only an affectionate disciplinarian but a most outstanding community leader. He has been a warm hearted and kindly friend of every boy and girl he has ever contacted. This is the type of person which is required for leadership in work with youth. Make no mistake, this is the priceless factor in the success of any such program. Bill Matus is a second Floyd Starr, the most outstanding leader in Youth Facility programs of America.

Many of Bill's original contacts with the Camp and its problems are most interesting. For instance, he was confronted with the "going business" problem of mechanical milking the 30 milk cows and attending to their feeding and care. For when we bought the farm we had to buy the cattle. So, practically overnight, with the help of a farm assistant, Bill learned to be a farmer, and particularly a dairyman. He was less successful with bull husbandry. One night the larger of the two prize bulls got on the rampage. He began destroying everything in his path. The Oxford police were called. They thought it quite funny at first until the bull charged them and struck their car. Fearfully these good police officers then drew their guns and shot the bull. So at this point in our program we then had a very expensive dead bull on our hands, only good for meat. Bill butchered the bull and put him up in cold storage and had meat for the boys for a long time. But it was very expensive meat, indeed!

# CHAPTER XII

# THE OAKLAND COUNTY
# BOARD OF SUPERVISORS

On our Board of Directors we placed two outstanding members of the Oakland County Board of Supervisors, Mr. William Ewart, City Attorney of Pontiac, and Mr. Clair Cummings, then head of the Savings and Loan of Pontiac. Also among our friends were many other Supervisors who had seen the program and become interested. Among them were David Levinson who was Chairman of the Ways and Means Committee, and Delos Hamlin, who was to become the fine Chairman of the Board of Supervisors. Oakland County had to make some pro-

DELOS HAMLIN
*Chairman Oakland County Board of Supervisors*

46

vision for the care of boys who were wards of the Juvenile Court which I then operated. It was not too difficult a job to sell the leaders of the Board of Supervisors and then the entire Board, by unanimous action, to provide the maintenance of the twenty boys who were assigned to Camp Oakland. So it was that we began operation of what was to be known as Boys' Ranch, a home for twenty homeless boys who had great need for home security.

Public officials will always aid children in need—if we only give them understanding of the need and importance of their assistance.

DAVID LEVINSON

*Chairman Ways and Means Committee, Oakland County Board of Supervisors and a Director of Camp Oakland Inc.*

47

HON. DONALD E. ADAMS
*Probate Judge, Oakland County*

PART II

# THE JUVENILE COURT
# AND
# NEW JUSTICE

# CHAPTER XIII

# LEADERSHIP IN PREVENTION

Today, Judges of all courts are leading the way in the prevention of crimes and juvenile delinquency. Both the law and the Courts have been hampered by antiquated concepts of criminal law and thus have been slow to progress toward prevention.

Formerly, children violating the law were treated as criminals just like adults. Then came the Juvenile Court. Here, the child was corrected rather than punished. This was a great step forward. But it still occurred too late. After he had erred in crime, often repeatedly. We now know we must aid the child before he is seriously injured morally.

So our modern Juvenile Court moves forward into the important field of prevention. This, the Judge himself must do, but only as an individual and a community leader, and not as a Court. Thus, the progressive Juvenile Court judge is:

1. An unofficial community leader of prevention; though offi- a Court of judiciously administered child treatment;

2. An efficient lawyer-judge protecting legal rights. His knowledge of the law is a prerequisite to both prevention and child assistance and care;

3. Part of the community team administering skilled and volunteer assistance to children.

All three are most important. But the most important is the Judge's position in the community in leadership toward prevention of Crime and Delinquency. For here, though he acts unofficially, he proceeds with all the power and persuasiveness of one who knows. The Court knows the criminal and delinquency problem better than any. Thus he forcefully advocates a simple truth—prevention is better than cure.

## What Shall the Judge Do?

Well knowing the truths concerning delinquency and neglect, the modern Juvenile Court Judges must be assertive. They must be civic leaders fighting the cause of youth against all neglects—emotional, physical, educational, cultural, moral and religious. For neglects of many types are the cause of delinquency.

Our society can no longer ignore the complicated facets of child neglect. They lie all about us. In truth, the trained judge must be a person able to clearly perceive these causes of neglect and delinquency, and deal with them.

A judge can no longer sit comfortably by, ignoring the unfortunate plight of neglected and delinquent children until formal complaint is made too late in the child's life. The Court cannot wait until children are repeatedly abused and perverted and then brought before the Court after moral turpitude and recidivism are in control.

Every judge feels the moral urge to do something about these children long before court. To help remove vicious and grievous child hazards. To prevent delinquency long before it has serious foothold; by early protection of children from these neglects.

Formerly judges succumbed to old fashioned legal arguments; that courts were:

(a) Purely forums for technical judicial proceedings;
(b) Solely to separate the good from the bad; right from wrong;
(c) Not to act as administrative agencies.

Thus the thoughtless judge may comfort his conscience, even today, by hiding behind these decrepit legal arguments. It is easy to practice punishment philosophies instead of samaritanism. Now they know better. The Juvenile Court has taught the way. The Criminal Court must follow.

In short, government must now begin most emphatically to prevent delinquency and immorality. Giving monetary or physical relief is no longer enough. Only by attention to these deeper problems of emotional, educational, cultural, religious and moral neglect may the children of the future be protected.

50

CHAPTER XIV

# PREVENTION MUST PRECEDE CRIME
## else it is
## JUSTICE SOUGHT TOO LATE

For these many years our Criminal Law has been blind and un-scientific. First, we have illogically insisted upon approaching Crime and Delinquency Prevention backwards. We have illogically insisted prevention can *follow* the offense. Second, we have blindly relied on the false remedy of punishment incarceration. We insist upon the out-dated theory "Punish him hard enough and he won't repeat". "Let the punishment fit the crime". "Strike back at the criminal". This is the vicious doctrine of blind vengeance. Sought to satisfy our frustrations over crime, blindly. Third, our false concept of freedom has defeated the scientific approach to human behavior. Legalistically and unscien-tifically we have insisted we could not attack crime until it has been committed. We have ignored both the character and need of the individual and his right to justice as a differing individual requiring individual understanding and treatment.

These fundamental errors must be met as follows:

(1) Prevention must necessarily *precede* crime;

(2) We must abandon punishment for vengeance. Use only correction;

(3) Justice must do more than merely determine technical guilt or innocence; it must admeasure the individual and satisfy his corrective needs.

The only path leading to both protection of the public and justice for the individual, is that of scientific reform of criminal process.

For years now, we have approached crime and delinquency through vengeance, frustration and animosity. Even our statutes have confused "prevention" and "correction". These are entirely different things. In-cidently, correction, no matter how good, is still a "too late" action.

51

We have clung to these errors because the legal profession is slow to make changes. Criminal law is still administered in the same old antiquated fashion. That is, we try the offense, not the individual. For instance, the prior criminal record of the respondent which enlightens his character is withheld from the jury. Only when he testifies may his record be shown and then only under the guise of determining his credibility. And we measure society's problem by archaic standards. We determine only guilt or innocense of one specific offense. Seldom do we ascertain the pressures and motivations behind the act. Forgiveness and mercy are theoretically absent from jury consideration. The law bends backwards to protect even the guilty from conviction. We We sacredly preserve the right to jury trial, the presumption of innocence, lawyers for indigents and restraints against unreasonable search and seizure. However, in the protective process many a guilty person goes free. Sometimes to sin more skillfully—more scornfully. On the other hand, nowhere do we review his total personality and character. We continue the old adages—an eye for an eye, etc.; let the punishment fit the crime. So each offense is punishable by an assumedly appropriate period of incarceration punishment. As if there were any real relationship between incarceration time and reformation of character. We require the Trial Judge to guess at the prognosis for future behavior, at the time of sentence, long before he is capable of correction. In all of this the inefficiency of blind emotionalism supercedes Judeo-Christian principles of helpfulness.

So, as we cling to this antiquated criminal penalistic system, it is no wonder we fail in prevention of crime. That is, no wonder that as we place emphasis solely on guilt or innocence of a single isolated law violation, we may miss justice. For determination of guilt of one solitary offense standing alone may solve little of the social problem.

Vengeful sadists urge us to "make an object lesson out of the criminal", saying, "then all persons will refrain from crime." What a false premise! For we commit or refrain from crimes because of our general and total characters—not from fear alone. We must separate correction and punishment from an entirely and distinct matter, namely prevention of crime.

Progressive indeed was the birth of the Juvenile Court in the beginning (1899) at Chicago, namely, in taking children out of the realm of criminal law. Splendid was the progress which followed—children were kept from jails and association with hardened criminals. Intelligent were the informal procedures and simplified rules of evidence. Most important, these were thus humanized to better learn and understand why the child misbehaved, as he did, and what caused the parental neglect. A kindly press has helped produce many of these innovations. The press has voluntarily withheld publication of childrens' names and identity, except when the public's interest demanded disclosure. Still all this has left much to be done.

There still remains to be consummated, "The New Justice for Children". The new justice for underprivileged; the new justice for children and families in need. This is a "Community-made" Justice for children. For the new justice, the community justice, is constituted of the community itself—of everyone and every influence in the community. Put these all together and you have the New Community Services for children—with a modern Juvenile Court to help where insistance or directive is needed. All are a part. All are necessary. This New Justice for children is also the story of Camp Oakland, Inc. and its services to children.

*Student Counselors and admirers*

HON. NORMAN BARNARD

*Judge of Probate and Juvenile Courts*

# CHAPTER XV

# THE MODERN JUVENILE COURT

The Juvenile Court is far ahead of criminal law, for several reasons.

*First—*

The child and his family look for help and know no punishment is involved.

*Second—*

This produces true, voluntary admissions of all the facts involved and permits the diagnostic analysis of the total social character and position of the child and his family. Confession of guilt is the rule in most cases. Because the caseworker can promise fair corrective treatment and assistance.

*Third—*

Planning toward better living under diagnosis of needs and with adequate supervision will immediately be begun. This is scientific and fruitful of moral success.

*Fourth—*and most important

Psychological testing and treatment immediately begun with the aid of psychiatry and under conditions like those of Camp Oakland, Inc. and its five programs—all this convinces the child and family that the Juvenile Court is really helpful and friendly. The crime is soon forgotten because it is overshadowed by the court's assistance.

So we must search for ways and means of advancing Juvenile Court services because they are so highly successful.

# CHAPTER XVI

# THE NEW JUVENILE COURT
## Provides New Justice For Children

### The Court Generally

Our general courts of justice were established to determine and adjudicate controversies. They protect the public by adjudicating criminal cases and sentencing the offenders. These courts were not originally intended as preventive agencies. Not until the advent of the Juvenile Court was it ever remotely suggested that courts might play an active part in the life of the community. But it was soon found that the Juvenile Court was most helpful, when cooperating with other services.

### Growth of the Juvenile Court

As legal skills have progressed we have come to realize that care, protection and treatment of both children and families is the object of Justice; that kindness and treatment are to be substituted for punishment. So we have learned that the chief function of the Juvenile Court is to serve underprivileged children. Consequently modern law has evolved the theory, tremendously important, that the Juvenile Court has not only a protective duty to society, but more important, a like protective duty of care, training and assistance to children and their families.

### Assist in Prevention

It is a short step from this duty to protect children and families to a much more important corollary duty; namely, that of preventing delinquency. If the Juvenile Court is to protect specific children who come to the court it is better that the court act as one of the cooperative agencies for the prevention of all delinquency. So our modern concept is that one of the chief functions of the Juvenile Court is to aid in the prevention of juvenile delinquency. Court preventive action is more important than Court treatment of the delinquent child.

Juvenile Court is Informal

*Juvenile Court Services—A Team of Services for Children*

The efficient Juvenile Court of today is not an individual judge, it is a staff of individuals. It is a combination—both a Court of Justice for children and an Agency for Family Assistance. It is not a legal minded Judge—it is a team of workers for children, including the Judge in charge.

Respect our "checks and balances" of the separate divisions of government as you will, yet there are necessary exceptions, one of which is required by the Juvenile Court.

Justice for children requires more than an adjudication concerning law violation, more than an equitable decree or mandate. Children, being unable to protect themselves, require continuing parental supervision and care. When natural parents are inadequate, the Juvenile Court must be a substitute parent over a considerable period of time, exercising much continuing care and supervision. Numerous persons must cooperate and diverse facilities must be coordinated to carry out the substitute parental obligations, as part of parental Juvenile Court.

Clinics must determine and administer to his emotional and mental needs, boarding parents act as foster parents, supervising caseworkers guide, assist and encourage. Parents must be assisted, educated and improved. Counsellors must advise and help plan for the future. All must show affection as they touch the child.

Many persons, working as a team, these are the component parts of the paternal Juvenile Court. They are the helping arms of the Court, the attentive ear, the observing eye, the clinical mind and the generous heart. The Judge, a lawyer interested in social needs, acts jointly through and with this team. Together—they are the component Juvenile Court.

This is new justice for children, provided in part by the Juvenile Court. Camp Oakland serves the Juvenile Court children and other underprivileged children of the county.

Boys' Ranch boys: Typical of many; whom we are very proud!

# CHAPTER XVII

# TOTAL COMMUNITY COOPERATION IS NEW JUSTICE

Here is the basic theory. Community Justice for children is a team work—a cooperative justice, the work, effort and accomplishment of all groups, agencies and people. None is dominant; each is supplemental. Who is engaged? Everyone—for no one in the community may be left out, or remove himself or avoid his part. Each of us has some responsibility to our community children. It is an opportunity, not obligation, to contribute a part towards the "New Justice for Children".

Opportunity yes indeed, for everyone, inherently and humanly desires to aid children—if he only knows how—and lo—here is how—simplified indeed!

So this is a story about children in need—and about you—helping them indeed in your own way and opportunity.

Somewhere in this story you will find described the work you yourself have done for youngsters.

I. W. Robertson, Vice President Camp Oakland and Chairman of Summer Camp Committee, tendering check by Birmingham High Twelve Club to William Matus for Camp Oakland.

*Entrance Childrens' Village*

*Counsellors are Listeners*

CHAPTER XVIII

# CHILDREN'S VILLAGE
## A Diagnostic Service Center for Needy Children and Youth

Judges Donald Adams and Norman Barnard of the Probate and Juvenile Court of Oakland County, deserve tremendous credit. For they have established what will ultimately be recognized as the most ideal court and service center for underprivileged children in America.

True to its name, Children's Village, Diagnostic and Service Center, is just what it describes. A friendly homelike village for children affording diagnosis and service to the children in need. It has now become a reality. The first three buildings, out of eight planned, are now in use.

Here any child or youth with emotional or behavior problems may be brought for instantaneous assistance. At once skilled specialists will apply their services to determine promptly what causes the symptoms, the misbehavior, the emotional or behavior pattern or other difficulties of the child or youth in need.

It is comparable in theory to prompt and early psychiatric diagnosis and care of mental hospitalization cases. It is designed to be both highly skillful and quickly effective. Kind care while the child is being studied will be accompanied by normal activities. Special schooling will follow achievement and emotion studies.

Psychologists, psychiatrists, counsellors and social caseworkers will rapidly analyze the child or youth, his personality, scholastic position, mental ability and emotional difficulties. Cultural, moral and religious deficiencies will be ascertained and evaluated.

There is immediate intake, prompt study and diagnosis, followed by court orientated or voluntary care programs. Short term intensive treatment care and training will soon supplant the old unscientific programs with their hopeless waiting lists, confused decisions and lack of scientific, correlated planning.

We use this same thorough plan in all good medical hospitalization. Why not afford the same skills to the child emotionally or morally sick? Why not rely upon skill and efficiency when dealing with children or youth with emotional or social problems?

Oakland County is to be congratulated upon this progressive program which its Board of Supervisors has established. Under the leadership of these most efficient Juvenile Court Judges Donald E. Adams and Norman R. Barnard.

# PART III

# PROTECTIVE SERVICES
# AND
# THE COMMUNITY

## Chapter XIX

# PROTECTIVE SERVICES
# PREVENTION OF DELINQUENCY

In every community there are pre-delinquent families and children. Families and their youngsters ripe for trouble, and soon to be brought before the authorities for neglect or delinquency. Everyone in the community knows this. Many facets of society, the schools, the police, the social agencies, the neighbors, know every predelinquent or neglected child. But in the past, they have all been silent, unwilling to tell what they know. Because they knew not whom to tell.

Trouble is we misunderstand the meaning of freedom. True kindness requires assistance for even those who reject or are afraid to trust necessary assistance. If we believe our religious teachings we will help these families, even a little against their will. How much better to aid a boy *before* he steals a car or breaks into a gas station or damages a building. To move in to help him and his family requires only a little moral courage and the simple skill of showing these underprivileged children and parents that:

(1) We like them.

(2) They need our help, and

(3) We have that ability to assist.

So to provide responsibility and available Prevention Programs, we have established a skilled Protective Service program in every com-

# PROTECTIVE SERVICE LEADERS

LEFT TO RIGHT—FRONT ROW:
Edgar Floor, *Supervisor;* Eugene Moore, *Chairman,* Birmingham; Edwin D. Phillips, *Chairman,* South Lyons; Judge Norman R. Barnard; Mrs. Virginia Yasaitis, *Chairman,* Lake Orion; Judge Donald E. Adams; Leon Avedesian, *Chairman,* Southfield; Robert Eddy, *Chairman,* Farmington; Andrew Althouse, *Chairman,* Oxford; James W. Hunt, *Director,* Children's Services; BACK ROW: Sherman LaMeasure, *Chairman,* Royal Oak.

65

munity. A Protective Service caseworker is located in each of our 25 cities, villages and townships. He is given a small headquarters office in the City Hall. By city ordinance, a committee of 25 citizens aids each worker in each city.

Confidential reports come to the committee or the caseworker from every conceivable source; the police, social agencies, the schools, neighbors and anyone who knows of the imminence of child or family disaster. Thus they learn of the approach of delinquency or neglect.

Then on an entirely confidential basis, the caseworker investigates.

A few complaints are unmerited. Most are more serious than realized. The result is the gathering of much pertinent predelinquency or neglect information.

A boy reportedly running the streets too late turns out to be a school truant, educationally retarded and a school failure, in broken home environment, without adequate supervision, without interest in any local youth activities, untruthful, of minor dishonesty. Perhaps his custodial parent is alcoholic or emotionally disturbed or just plain inadequate.

With this picture drawn clear by proper investigation, the skillful caseworker candidly but kindly offers and urges assistance. Obtains child guidance, or family service, or visiting teacher, or school tutoring, or a job, or necessary clothes, or Alcoholic Anonymous or psychiatric service for the parent.

After these steps have begun, then the community offers its warm personal assistance and service. A small boy can be furnished a Big Brother who will truly care; or furnished a membership in the Y.M.C.A. or the local Boys' Club or in Scouting or in a Church Club.

Today in Oakland County hundreds of such children and families are being helped by their own community, by social agencies, by their schools, by churches, by youth organizations, to again feel they are worthwhile. That they have friends and acquaintances who truly care.

CHAPTER XX

# EMOTIONAL AND OTHER NEGLECT

New Justice is necessarily one of Prevention and Protection instead of Punishment.

*Leadership in Preventing*

Today Juvenile Courts are seizing leadership. They are acting to prevent child abuse and delinquency.

But court reform is slow, for we have been hampered by antiquated legal tradition. For a long time it was deemed necessary to keep the juvenile courts out of the field of prevention of delinquency. The first Juvenile Court was beneficially designed to assist the child. But unfortunately only after he had failed or erred sufficiently to be a court ward. Though this was better than criminal justice, it was still obviously help coming too late. So the modern Juvenile Court Judges have learned they must move forward into the field of prevention. Of course they must do so as individuals not as courts. Thus our Juvenile Court Judges now recognize and face the following truths:

*Emotional Neglect—*

Emotional neglect being intangible, is difficult to describe, hard to prove and often overlooked. Consequently, too often the law thus ignored or avoided its impact. This left us with many emotionally deprived and abused children. They then grew up with perverted minds, distorted personalities, and deviated behavior.

For instance, take the child who has been emotionally beaten back and forth between vicious, fighting parents. Such a child is often treated as a shuttlecock in their marital vituperations, recriminations, and animosity. Many such pathetic children I have known —searching everywhere for security and affection—soon afraid to trust anyone. Truly emotionally psychopathic.

67

## Moral Neglect—

Moral neglect has been sadly overlooked or condoned. Simply because its effect is not easily traced as the proximate cause of delinquency.

Take such children I have known. One came from a morally improverished home. Degraded by a superficially loving mother selfishly living by prostitution. When the age of understanding came, this youngster necessarily lost both parental and self respect. With this the child soon felt forced to reject all morality.

Consider another child I have known. He grew up midst criminal parents and older sibling delinquents. The father was an oft repentent common thief, though too seldom caught. A large family of older children became law violators as rapidly as they grew old enough. Small chance in this home environment. This lad soon went the same way.

## Physical Neglect—

To often physical neglect goes excused or unreported. In many other cases physical neglect; namely, brutality, or lack of food, clothing or shelter though present are accompanied by emotional or moral neglect in the background. Careful search may exhibit both physical and other neglect.

## Educational Neglect—

How may we attack educational neglect? The schools have small chance of success where parental apathy or opposition predominates. For instance, another child I knew came from an educationally deprived and depreciating home. Here all education in general and the schools in particular were continuously berated, criticized and scorned.

Naturally this youth, though of good mentality, became first a school drop-out, next a resultant malcontent and ultimately a car thief.

Compulsory education is needed. We must mandate education through high school or 20 years of age. Only by such national law will inadequate parents cooperate.

## Cultural Neglect—

Children may also be sadly neglected culturally, ethically and religiously. Every person needs these. I am reminded of a bright youth, emotionally impoverished through lack of cultural contacts, religious training and ethical precept. He grew up a selfish animal deviate and thief with no feeling for others. Naturally he became anti-social, a crafty, cheating, deceitful, habitual law violator.

*Our first swimming hole*

# Chapter XXI

# DELINQUENCY IS INHERITED

Delinquency in a family reproduces itself! The delinquency of the parents is usually transmitted to the children. To help the child, you must help the whole family.

Such parents unintentionally furnish the delinquency environment and background for their children. Love them—they surely do; but help them, they cannot—without much insistent community assistance.

The good people of each community do try to help such parents, try to direct them to church, into good recreation, to guidance clinics, to family service associations and counselling, and toward other community services. Unfortunately most of them are unwilling and recidivistic. Left to themselves they reject community services and sink back in the quagmire of ignorance and bad habit from which they have come. Consequently many such parents seem to be a lost cause.

We search for new resources. What may our community do about such persons? Now if they would voluntarily accept the help of the available services in any community, much could be done to assist them to help themselves. It is true, some do see the light and attempt to improve their lives. Unfortunately, most refuse because we, the so-called "good people" of the community have failed to befriend and assist them adequately: therefore, they are free to continue in selfishness and ignorance. So they go on to relative degrees of crime—and human degradation.

Their pain and misery should challenge us as "Brothers' Keepers" but we seldom see the details of their troubles—we only see their evil shadow. Somehow we must learn to induce them to improve their lives even against their own ignorant will.

The only hope is for earlier community services when families are very young; for mandatory help if necessary to those reluctant to use assistance. Kindly, insistent, enforced help is often the best form of guidance under the circumstances:

(1) This means assertive "Protective Services" in every community.

(2) It means religious and moral training for all.

(3) It requires steady jobs and full work opportunities.

(4) It requires improved parents and stronger families.

CHAPTER XXII

# CHARACTERISTICS OF DELINQUENTS

Most of the families coming to the Juvenile Court have withdrawn from or been rejected by their community. They do not live in the healthy channels of normal community life. Study and tabulation of youngsters appearing before our Juvenile Court show the following common characteristics:

CHARACTER TRAITS
OF 300 DELINQUENT AND NEGLECTED CHILDREN COMING TO
THE JUVENILE COURT AS TABULATED BY CASEWORKERS

NUMBER

| | |
|---|---|
| 286 | Lack religious training and church attendance |
| 279 | Have no membership or participation in children's clubs or organizations |
| 179 | Have no active participation in athletics |
| 178 | Dislike school |
| 145 | Show unwholesome use of leisure time |
| 141 | Have no hobbies |
| 138 | Come from broken homes |
| 127 | Have poor father-child relationship |
| 118 | Have poor parental supervision |
| 118 | Show retarded reading level |
| 99 | Are unreliable and dishonest |
| 92 | Have inadequate family income |
| 70 | Dislike their home |
| 69 | Possess low I.Q. or low achievement |
| 69 | Have poor mother-child relationship |
| 50 | Have parents who are in poor health |
| 44 | Have poor peer relationship |
| 41 | Have poor sibling relationship |
| 30 | Suffer from unfair parental treatment |
| 26 | Have poor health |
| 23 | Have poor step parent-child relationship |
| 12 | Have early abnormal sex experience |

Note that lack of religious training and church attendance heads the list of characteristics. This should give us a simple clue to the

71

religious and moral training needed by these underprivileged families.

Next come non-membership in youth groups, no athletic participation, lack of hobbies and the unwholesome use of leisure time. Here again, simple ingredients of good community life could readily be made available to each underprivileged child, through such youth groups and recreation.

The failure of the family entity is shown by broken homes, poor father-child relationship and by the poor, but somewhat better mother-child relationship.

Unreliability and dishonesty are by-products of poor parental care. Poor peer and sibling relationship, and unfair parental treatment result from untrained and inadequate parents.

Broken homes demand better marriages. This diminishes divorce.

Inadequate family income should challenge our interest in minimum wage laws and adequate annual earnings. It is tough sledding to be a good parent with inadequate means. Families must have jobs!

Failure of school adjustment and inability to read furnishes a great challenge toward improved personalized education. Forty percent of our youth are "drop outs" without finishing high school.

Low on the list comes mental inadequacy. Our psychologists believe some share of this is really social ignorance.

Parental and child health demand more attention.

Step parents do better than we think!

Early sex misbehavior is not overly important.

So careful analysis supports these simple conclusions:

1. Steady work is vital.
2. Better training for parentage and family life is a necessity.
3. Involvement in Good Community Living is requisite.
4. Religious and Moral Training are most important.

*Camp Oakland belongs to our children. This they feel, understand and believe*

# Chapter XXIII

# PREVENTION BY PROTECTION— THE GREAT OBJECTIVE

Prevention is always better than cure. We all know preventive medicine as our greatest protector. It is the safeguard of public health. But what protection have we from delinquency; the contagious social illness?

Statistics show that from two to four percent of our children are suffering predelinquency. But this percentage does not represent our total problem. All of these children with such personal problems influence the behavior pattern and happiness of the other 96 percent to a great degree.

To usually get caught in misbehavior and to face treatment discipline regularly is great prevention therapy for every child. But to prevent misbehavior, both parents and the community must know about it and accept full responsibility.

Now, were 4 percent of our children suffering from any other contagious disease such as smallpox or typhoid fever, preventive steps would be taken. Living in fear of epidemic, we would establish a health agency with full responsibility. Such a public health committee would correlate all of the facilities of the community to eradicate the contagious health menace.

We have so well attacked the problem of protecting our children's physical health that many diseases are no longer existent, and others are negligible. TB is regulated and will be controlled completely in our lifetime. Preventive medicine has shown the way to better health. Delinquency may be prevented in much the same way.

We prevent illiteracy! Let us look at our public school system. It is common, accepted public view that all of our children must be educated. Compulsory education is fully accepted law. Not just 90 percent or 96 percent but 100 percent—to the degree that they are educable.

Delinquency is a social disease—equally contagious and dangerous. But unlike public health, or public education, when we deal with delinquency we do not insist upon prevention. We do not attack the cause. We permit its contagion to flourish and treat its victims too late. We have no goal. We follow no plan. We have no agency responsible for delinquency eradication. We say we have not the right to interfere in other people's lives. We are told we cannot mandate morals. So we have succumbed to the false doctrine that we cannot prevent delinquency.

Laxity concerning contagion will not be permitted, but we seem to forget that delinquency menaces children's mental, emotional and moral health just as seriously. So our public concept of contagious dangers to children should be broadened. We must insist that delinquency be prevented 100 percent; in the case of all children and of all families. Its contagion should be prevented at its source and inception. Correction, after social illness, delinquency and neglect have left their mark—this is "too little too late!" This is a community responsibility primarily on a local level. Thus, prevention begins in a community's conscience and willingness to establish and support a preventive agency with full responsibility to correlate all resources and to do the job.

*Clinical Psychologists—analyze character*
*Then treatment and care may be successful*

# Chapter XXIV

# DELINQUENT HERITAGE

## Who Are Criminals?

To many persons, friends, neighbors, and even some teachers, the delinquent youngster is just a bad boy. He is often nice looking, and attractive though untrained or unfortunate. But he is potential criminal dynamite!

Much confusion exists about what delinquency and crime really are. Unfortunately, many people visualize the average criminal as the brilliant safecracker or vicious thug of television. Others describe him as the youth who should be excused his misdeeds because of his poor character training.

In truth the average criminal is ignorant, selfish, mentally inept and socially inadequate. His skills consist of falsehood, deceit, and dishonesty. He is a confused, thwarted and defeated individual. Usually he is mentally disturbed and emotionally unhappy. He is largely socially rejected long prior to his latest crime. If he steals, it is because he lacks will power and foolishly thinks he won't be caught. If he rapes, it is because his concept of sex is perverted. If he kills, it is usually the result of fear.

If we keep this true picture of the criminal in mind, we shall better understand the predelinquent's needs, and better how to help him.

## Background of Delinquency

Inadequate parents, the untrained, the unreliable, and the immoral continually bring more underprivileged children into the world. Most of these inadequate parents, whether married or single, at first possess some affection for each other. Love, either crude or refind, is a great foundation for stable family life. Cupid helps the most inadequate lovers, that is, if accompanied by some virtues of character. Unfortunately, most of these parents were themselves underprivileged, and lacking in the basic requirements for parentage. Thus character qualifications ar inadequate or entirely lacking.

Consequently it is often true that at some stage of their family living, for the welfare of the children there must come the mandate of the community through the Juvenile Court. Society belatedly insists they must behave better or they will lose their children. Unfortunately, this mandate usually comes too late—after years of abuse of children and after repetitious family misconduct. Too often the girl of the family runs the streets, runs away, becomes pregnant, abortion is sought or child marriage. Thus the vicious circle has been completed by running its entire course. The new generation has grown up from the inadequate background of the previous one. A new cycle has begun. Delinquency truly perpetuates itself.

*Counsellors are Friends with understanding and affection as well as advice*

# CHAPTER XXV

# REACHING PREDELINQUENCY

How may we reach predelinquency? How shall we find the child in need? What may we do for him? We must be both realistic and scientific in our approach. The solution is intricate. Many skills must contribute. Numerous agencies must help. But above all, the elimination of delinquency must be a popular objective. The community, the school, the Church, the clinics, the agencies, the youth facilities, the police; each of these can contribute. But the public, you and I the ordinary citizen, must fervently desire and willingly assist.

*Community Services*

Excellent planning for children and families makes provision for a wide range of welfare services and activities in nearly every community. These include the familiar pattern of churches, schools, health services, the police, family counselling, child welfare services, recreational facilities and public assistance. There are many special services to families, such as financial aid, special education, clinical health service, psychological and psychiatric consultation and treatment, advice on family problems and marital difficulties, day care for children, foster care and many others.

*These services are open to anyone—that is anyone who asks for them and is willing to receive them. These are the services the unfortunate of America reject and are permitted to do without—when their need is the greatest. Our big job is to get the family to the service! Their cooperative assistance will reach and treat all children with such problems, if, but only if, their work is coordinated.*

*Locate the Child and his Problem*

Our first step toward helping the predelinquent is to find him and learn about his problem. If we are attentive, we all see him every day —on the street, in the movies, at the store, or in school. If we care about his welfare, we can observe the symptoms and pass our knowledge on to skilled persons who in turn will know what to do. This is, of course, if we have such skilled persons. But, better still we can pass our observations on to our Child Protection Agency—if we have one!

Oakland County has a child protection service in every community.

*Learn the Symptoms*

The public should know the more readily discernible signs of delinquency, the symptoms of child trouble—and utilize this knowledge.

Generally speaking, any behavior which offends our concept of proprieties may be cause for concern, any breach of law, any dishonesty or immoral behavior may be important. Indications of cruelty, excessive hatred or animosity, wanton disregard of others, or evidence of unhappiness or loneliness are equally to be observed. None of these may be important in the life of the particular child, because other good factors may be dominantly corrective. But we should be concerned and attentive, in a kindly way, to the symptoms of every child we meet, otherwise we cannot help.

For instance, when a small boy behaves improperly, patient, kindly questioning should always ensue. This may bring a response showing remorse and good training; or on the other hand, a disrespectful retort exhibiting ignorance, selfishness, lack of discipline or proper training. Improper attitudes are always cause for concern. Behavior symptoms should never be ignored. Parents should always be apprised and if they seem careless, then the police or the Visiting Teacher should be contacted. We never help a child by ignoring his needs.

*Schools Prevent Delinquency*

If we give proper support to our schools, they will work insistently toward preventing delinquency. Children's problems exhibited at school often disclose the primary symptoms.

Strict regularity of school attendance is paramount to most children's learning.

Some parents foolishly permit their children to remain out of school. He who loses considerable elementary schooling this year may fail next year for lack of fundamentals.

Juvenile Court records show that on an average, delinquent and neglected children are invariably educationally retarded in achievement by nearly two school grades; they function below both their normal school grade and also below their own intelligence quotient. For instance, the delinquent 14-1/2 years of age with an I.Q. of 94 may be found in the 7th grade instead of the eighth, but actually by achievement test, prove to be functioning at fifth grade reading level, sixth grade spelling and fourth grade arithmetic ability.

79

CHAPTER XXVI

# THE DEFICIENT CHILD DESERVES "NEW JUSTICE"

Delinquent children are always so because they are permitted to be deficient educationally, morally, culturally and emotionally. These deficiency handicaps must be overcome. Take educational failure. Even though the child be somewhat slow in learning, by supporting help, his achievement may be brought right up to his proper elementary grade level. Some home work or special school help or remedial assistance will do the job.

Now think what this means to him. Being an eighth grade student with eighth grade ability, he is supposed to recite and participate. Suppose he is asked to read aloud, he stumbles over the words; his classmates laugh; he is chagrined and embarrassed. He must fight humiliation somehow. What may he do? Perhaps he becomes a listless dullard and refuses to be hurt further by class activity; perhaps he adopts a bellicose attitude to warn people to "keep off" him, or perhaps he misbehaves, makes noise, breaks the rules, disrupts the school routine so he may "show them he is important anyway." Perhaps he picks fights, insults the girls, caricaturizes the teacher or exposes vulgarity. Possibly he breaks into the school or other building at night and is destructive. All these and many other devices are his methods of handling this problem. They are for protection, recognition or to strike back. He utilizes them because he is fearful, defeated or resentful. Being selfish helps him use them wilfully.

Society used to misunderstand and tried to solve his misbehavior solely by punishment. Now we know better. We turn him over to the remedial reading teachers, find a class he can "measure up" in, ask his parents to cooperate and help with home work. We forgive him; induce him to like us and cooperate; but insist that he behave well, with punishment as a known but unused last resort.

80

*Help by Other Youth is New Justice*

Here a great opportunity for help by other youngsters may be missed. Youths are so unrelenting, so unkind, when they do not understand the personal problem or background of their associates. They punish the underprivileged mercilessly when they should be friendly. If they but understand they would willingly assist.

A wise teacher will explain and gain student support and acceptance instead of derision and rejection—if she has the time and training.

Most of all—teachers are overloaded and usually too busy to help as much as they would like. They have the superhuman task of providing individual education to an oversized heterogeneous group; a class which includes brilliant, ordinary and slow learning students— all with the same program. What a task! Actually these "problem youngsters" should be scholastically separated by bus transportation if necessary into a classroom of youngsters with like needs. Shallcross School of Philadelphia does exactly that!

*The Child's Personal Symptoms*

Children show their own personal problems by behavior, conversation and attitudes. Schools come close to children and may readily observe these every day. Both careful observance of symptoms and appropriate action are imperative. They see the overly aggressive child, th fearful, seculsive youngster; they catch the lack of hearing, the difficulty of sight, the lack of physical controls, the violence of temper, the unusual fluctuations of temperament, the lack of consideration, the immoral or crude behavior. They observe nearly all sides of the child's personality. They do their best to control, guide, correct and improve. And here is the point—if these symptoms are severe or numerous or if they still meet failure after a reasonable period of effort such as a school semester, they must immediately ask for skilled help!

*Symptoms of Parental Neglect*

On the other hand, when the teacher first sees substantial evidence of parental child neglect or mistreatment, say in the first grade—this is the time to immediately take action. The Visiting Teacher should be apprised—she will know how to follow the symptoms through to their cause, will have tact to contact parents and gain their appreciative cooperation rather than their opposition.

She will also know how to withdraw silently when the seeming symptoms of child trouble are actually only incidents of normal behavior.

*Symptoms Observed by Police*

Police are chief observers. They see youngsters on the street, in the stores and in public places. To them is reported all manner of child misbehavior. Here is another great access to children's problems. Kindly, insistent questioning will show much of the child's personality —may indicate much help is needed or no action warranted. But most of all, this information learned, if serious, should always be passed on to both the parents and the school or the appropriate child protection agency of the community. This will not harm the child if the facts are held in strict confidence. Actually the purpose is to assist both the child and his family.

If your child misbehaves—say slightly, would you not like to know? Will you not welcome the assistance of the schools when they stand ready to help solve the problem, however slight? Yes indeed.

## Symptoms Observed by Others

Ordinary citizens see much overt misbehavior. The ten year old smoking, petty theft, children loitering late at night. We hear indecent language, see discourtesy and witness abusive mistreatment of others. Too often we ignore the possible problem and do nothing. This is indeed wrong. If the misbehavior is serious though slight, the information should be passed on to parents—they are entitled to know. We should take the time to contact them in a friendly way. If the misbehavior is very serious, the parents, the police and the school should all be advised. They may all be of help. Here is the advantage of an organized child protection program. A central office system can take reports, tabulate information and keep all helpful community agencies alert where necessary. It can provide better secrecy protection than any other agency—if desirable. On the other hand, it can help police and school and other agencies in many ways. It will give assistance to the child long before vicious recidivistic habits are acquired. Casework may be done much earlier, when success is much more likely. Symptoms, like temper tantrums, if attended may prevent violent injuries later in life. Disrespect and insolence do not need to grow into delinquency or mental illness. Petty falsehood and dishonesty, if promptly treated, need not mature into felonious crime.

## The Visiting Teacher or Social Worker—Serves New Justice

The social work toward such delinquency prevention or child protection may be performed by any skilled worker. I have suggested a trained staff member of the Juvenile Court acting for a local committee. A Visiting Teacher will serve equally as well or any other skilled children's caseworker, provided he is given authority and cooperation.

82

In many localities the Visiting Teacher is available and best able to serve. What shall she do about the family in question? How long shall she continue? How insistent may she be? When shall she refer all or part of the given problem on to others such as the Family Service Association, the Child Guidance Clinic, the State Mental Hospital Clinic, or the Juvenile Court?

## Screening and Diagnosis

Perhaps the most difficult function in all child welfare services is that of ascertaining the needs of an individual child or family and finding the particular services which will best serve that need.

## Diagnostic Service is required for New Justice

So the "key" duty in this entire program is that placed upon the investigating case worker; that of investigation and diagnosis of the needs of the individual child or family. It is tremendously important that families who can stand on their own feet be left entirely within their own resources. Ordinary family quarrels, and many other family problems do not contribute materially to delinquency or show any need for predelinquent consideration. Thus, it is most important to first screen out the complaints which are not meritorious and not to infringe upon any personal liberties of the family involved.

Such screening brings difficulty of determining which community services may best be utilized.

Are there physical factors needing attention? Is the misbehavior indicative of basic injury? Is the child retarded in school because of inherent mental retardation or through emotional blockage, or resulting from loss of early educational opportunities? Are the services of the Visiting Teacher or the school counsellor or the Child Guidance Clinic necessary or sufficient in the given case? Is the child to be referred for psychological tests or special education? Should the family be helped by the Family Service Association? Is conference with a religious leader important? Is psychiatric counselling warranted? Are the mental and emotional problems severe so as to require in-patient or out-patient mental hospitalization? These and a multitude of similar questions arise in proper screening after case investigation.

Doctor L. Jerome Fink, Pontiac Psychiatrist, and the Oakland County Medical Society Mental Health Committee, gives the following statement to aid in observing symptoms and making referrals.

"There are three basic areas in which a child's behavior is identified as either normal or abnormal. These are: 1. The school. 2. The home. 3. The neighborhood. A child who is having difficulty in his adjustment reaction in one area only, i.e., the school situation alone, should be cause for concern. However, in his adjustment is poor in two of the above mentioned areas this should be considered a serious behavior problem. If all three areas are involved the child's emotional difficulties should be considered as very severe.

Obviously, the protective service caseworker, visiting teacher or the social worker, should have the initial involvement with all children having superficial problems academically or within the school area. If this problem continues to appear to be of a superficial nature then it should continue to be the visiting teacher who works with the situation. If, however, the visiting teacher makes no progress with the situation over a six month period, this, in itself, should be an indication for referral to a Child Guidance Clinic.

If after an initial investigation in which the visiting teacher takes a brief history and visits the home, only to discover that the problem is more complex than was originally ascertained, this should be an indication for Family Service or Child Guidance Clinic referral. In this event once per week visits to the home by the worker or clinic should be done for the purpose of visiting with the parents and further evaluating the problem. The visiting teacher should be free to play an important part in the screening and referral role.

In the event that more serious signs and symptoms occur, then psychiatric out-patient clinic and hospital examinations would be indicated. Here is a scale showing the visual symptoms which a visiting teacher, or other social worker, should look for, find, and depend upon in determining where to send a given child for referral. It starts with problems which should case concern and increases in magnitude to problems which are obviously of a very severe nature.

1. There may be academic failure of the child.
2. Or irregular school attendance.
3. Stealing, if persistent after attempted correction, is very important. Although certain types are not too serious since they are merely a phase of development of the younger child.
4. Symptoms of withdrawal and seclusiveness in the classroom, in social groups, in the school setting, or from the peer group in the neighborhood, are important.
5. Repeated desires of unusual behavior in unrealistic settings, such as Masturbation; or repeated unusual sex behavior.
6. Disruption of classroom by hostile, aggressive acting out toward the teachers or toward other children.
7. Tears, anger, terror, jealousy of an extreme degree.

8. Hallucinations, irrational behavior, delusions, the disoriented child who is psychotic.

Obviously, in the last instance on the scale there should be no question but that this child should be immediately referred for psychiatric out-patient hospital examination, and no time lost by the visiting teacher or the Child Guidance Clinic prior to such referral."

Thus, the lead in this matter and the primary duty of referral judgment lies entirely in the hands of the social worker, whether he be a member of the staff of the Juvenile Court or a Visiting Teacher or attached to the Child Protection Committee. The greatest skill is none too good!

*Small children need love, guidance and training: To them story time is very necessary*

# Chapter XXVII

# PREVENTION BY POLICE—
# AIDS NEW JUSTICE

*Duty of the Police Department*

The police department exists in every community for protection; to apprehend law violators and criminals. It is not primarily a preventive agency, but it does great protective work. It is also most helpful in its modern educational and safety programs. Yet it is not alone the source to which we may look to prevent children from becoming delinquent. The police department is not employed as an agency to prevent family difficulties, or to train children. However, it is of immeasurable help in Protection, Preventive and Educational Service when joined with other community activities. Its opportunity for finding the child with a problem or need is second only to the teachers. Prompt police referral is most important.

# Chapter XXVIII

# CHURCH RESPONSIBILITY
# FOR NEW JUSTICE

For over 30 years I have dealt with the needs and problems of improverished peoples—children, youth and families. These in need, seldom are in great want of physical things—food, clothing and housing. Theirs is generally the lack of emotional, education and cultural needs, more even than health needs.

In our land of abundance these children, youth and families are sadly lacking much more important requisites—self-discipline, religious training, moral courage and straight thinking ability. Most are poor, but some are of rich families. They are the product of stagnated communities and morbid social cultures. Most face further impoverishment through wanning job opportunity or their own low horizons. Tomorrow only the alert, the educated and the self disciplined will be able to compete in our new highly scientific economy.

What part has the church in this changing world? Now we know these small children are being cultivated into emotional disturbance, immorality, and delinquency.

But is this a matter for the church goer?

We, the good church people of America do not run in contact with them. We do not know their problems, nor realize the depth of their problems.

Why should we be concerned? Are they a responsibility of religion?

Isn't 2 to 10 percent of our church budget spent on so-called missionary work or church extension?

Well the answer is simple. All good of morality springs from religion. It is so in history and the simple truth will so remain. A great upsurge in religious action for child welfare is eminent. This is a religious obligation, far beyond present activity.

# Chapter XXIX

# RELIGIOUS ASSISTANCE
## *is Protective Justice*

Parents teach their children by self-example.

When a small boy sees his parents cheating each other, reflecting vicious hatreds and observes their dishonesty and falsehood, such a lad has a difficult choice to make indeed. He must live in their custody and with the parents, so the problem is great. He has two choices—

First, since he is to tied to the vicious parent, will he feel compelled to follow his malicious pattern and example? And ultimately behave badly just like the poor parent? or

Second, shall he have the wisdom to understand the parents misbehavior, forgive his misdeeds, but though still loving the parent, refuse to follow his bad example?

To follow this latter course, children need religious training. They need to understand Christ's teachings. To turn the other cheek. How to forgive 70 times 7. The words, "Forgive them for they know not what they do!" The beauty of the 23rd Psalm and the wisdom of the Ten Commandments should be understood. The story of the Talents gives understanding.

Over half of America's children have no religious training. These include the delinquent and neglected. How may we improve young America without religious training and its moral and spiritual culture?

So it was that we sought the aid of our county churches, Protestant, Catholic, Jewish. Five hundred clergy responded. They offered to welcome every such underprivileged youngster who was willing to attend their church.

Ray Herrick of Tecumseh gave $10,000, and community leaders, Samuel J. Lang, U. S. Bratton, Jr., Ike Robertson, Walter Gehrke, "Shorty" Snyder, Bob Critchfield, Rodger Emmert, Robert Vander-Kloot, Walter Anderson, Henry M. Hogan, Sr., George Averill, Bill Troutfetter, Bill Arlund, and John Maynard raised another $10,000 just one morning at breakfast.

With over $20,000 to begin, we hired a famous ball player, Hal Newhouser, who is a clean, splendid young idol of youth. Hal would seek out a boy and his parent, whom a local Protective Service Committee wished to gain religious training and community acceptance. Simple enough; most youngsters would do anything to be with Hal Newhouser.

So in his company they would meet the clergyman of the church of his parents' choice. Once made at home, such a lad gained both religious or Sunday school training and also new friends of the right sort.

Religious assistance and church acceptance for youth is part of the Protective Assistance every community should offer its predelinquent and neglected children.

Of such is the kingdom of heaven; 'tis the greatest service a church may render.

*Work-Education Camp Boys*
*Every boy must now have training and education*
*However religious assistance is equally important*

89

# CHAPTER XXX

# DIVORCE AND THE BROKEN HOME— JUSTICE DEFEATED

Family disintegration, divorce and the broken home cause most delinquency and child neglect.

We must rapidly reduce this cause by giving our children home security. The rights of children to adequate homes and parents has long been denied these children.

This is the age of challenge to American family life. Most of today's youth have higher standards, seek greater attainments and accomplish more than the youth of any previous generation. They study and try harder to be scientists, engineers, business managers and professionals. They now seek a college education, and many attend graduate schools. These are our future leaders. They are splendid, indeed!

But there is the other extreme—that of our lethargic, undisciplined, licentious youth. These are the lazy drop-outs, the cheap gangs, the "free thinkers." They are rebellious, disloyal and bad citizens. They are nurtured on the slogans, "give me my rights," "the government owes me," "why work hard?" Here lies America's Achilles heel—our wasted youth, our atrophied asset.

It is high time we begin to make these youth into good Americans. But to do so, we need a religious crusade for morality, self-discipline and integrity. We face a great educational job for mandatory learning —but made more interesting and more practical. We need a national program for full upgrading of youth horizons. Stop gap programs are useless. CCC camps just to keep youngsters off the streets without educating them are a losing endeavor.

*Strong Home Life*

But most of all, the integrity, sanctity and basic values of home life must be strengthened, fortified and respected. For the failure of the inadequate home is the basic cause of youth without character. So better marriages with less divorce and broken homes—here lies the solution.

It is significant that at least half of the cases of child delinquency or neglect are accompanied by parental separation.[1] Broken marriages are usually the product of unreliable, ill-trained or inadequate parents.[2] Fellow judges, lawyers and social workers all agree that children of divorce and separation are usually insecure and emotionally disturbed.

## About Marriage

These facts about marriage are most important:

a. In most states there are practically no standards, qualifications, training or other prerequisites for marriage and parentage,[3] other than blood tests for venereal disease.

b. Though our religious schools furnish some marital education, marriage training and education for family living is rarely taught in the public schools. Good family training by example and experience is afforded half of our children, but the balance receive none.

c. There are no practical, legal safeguards to prevent the mental or socially inadequate and the emotionally disturbed from being married.[4]

d. The immoral and the emotionally disturbed have full legal right to marry. They do so with impunity. Their offspring suffer accordingly, by inheriting these deficiencies.

e. Inadequate marriages produce many divorces and family separations, usually leaving the children without adequate home security.

f. Marriages of such inadequate parents produce an ever-increasing share of inadequate, insecure and emotionally disturbed children.

g. For instance, each year in Michigan, about 2,100 socially inadequate, pregnant unmarried girls, usually under the age of consent and without moral stamina or character requisites for successful marriage, are authorized to marry secretly.[5] In return, the plight of their unfortunate children is sad and dismal indeed.

## About Illegitimate Children

a. About seventy-two hundred illegitimate births occur annually in Michigan.[6] Compartively few of these children are adopted or legitimatized by marriage.[7]

---

[1]Michigan Juvenile Court Reports
[2]Agreed hypothesis by judges and courtworkers dealing with children and families
[3]See M.S.A. 25.2 et. seq.
[4]M.S.A. 25.6 has no enforcement provisions
[5]Statewide estimate projected from Oakland County figures
[6]1960 figures used for estimate
[7]Compared to adoption figures

b. There are about 130,000 illegitimate children in Michigan.[8]
c. Most of these illegitimate children are brought up by their own inadequate mothers under the traumatic cloud of social stigma, and ignorant of the needs for adequate child care.
d. It is estimated that nearly $10 million a year of A.D.C. money goes to support socially or legally illegitimate children in Michigan.[9]
e. These children are subject to social rejection, emotional disturbance, the handicap of family insecurity and ignorance.

*About Divorce*

a. Divorce and separation strike the homes of about 25.6 percent of Michigan's children.[10] Some few divorces may actually be helpful to the children involved. But most divorces work great emotional insecurity and trauma upon the children.
b. There are between 300,000 and 500,000 children of divorce under divorce court supervision in Michigan.[11]
c. Thus it is estimated that from eight to thirteen million American children are wards of the divorce courts in the United States—more than the total population of Michigan.[12]
d. Casework assistance to these children is negligible. The volume is so great as to make it practically impossible—based on Wayne and Oakland County figures there are between 4,000 and 5,000 children of divorce for every divorce court social caseworker.
e. Broken homes are invariably abnormal, lacking in security, and hazardous to the children. They often cause children serious frustration and emotional disturbances.[13] Moral and emotional neglect as well as delinquency may ensue.[14] Crime follows as a natural result.
f. The State of Michigan supplements alimony payments by welfare or A.D.C.; sometimes both.[15] This financial assistance does not, of itself, prevent moral and emotional neglect; and necessary casework to this end is admittedly inadequate.
g. Based on Oakland County figures, nearly $10 million of alimony supplementation is paid annually by A.D.C. and welfare throughout

[8]Estimated from 1964 figures
[9]Estimates only—from reliable sources
[10]Based on Wayne and Oakland County figures
[11]Estimated from 1960 Wayne and Oakland County figures
[12]Estimated from Michigan figures
[13]Michigan Juvenile Reporting System
[14]Acknowledged by caseworkers and courts.
[15]See Welfare and Bureau Social Aid Law and Regulations

Michigan. This estimate comes from the figures of Oakland County which has 9 percent of the state population.[16]

h. Defaulting—nonpaying parents are free to remarry. This causes the state to carry more and more of the burden. These defaulters bring more children into the world and compound the non-support obligation.

These being the facts—what are we to do? There are several useful steps to be taken.

First: The sanctity, importance and permanence of marriage must be reaffirmed. This may be done by:

(a) All religious marriages requiring training or counseling as a prerequisite.

(b) Non-religious marriages requiring marital training and educational requirements.

Second: Divorce should be prohibited in all cases except where—

(a) There are no children under 18 years, or

(b) The divorce is proven necessary for the welfare of the children.

Third: No marriage should be permitted where the parties are defaulted in alimony or unable to sustain their present family obligations.

Fourth: All illegitimate children should automatically receive court protective service to make certain they are either well cared for or placed for adoption.

---

[16]In October, 1961, 567 divorce cases in Oakland County were supplemented as follows:

| | | |
|---|---|---|
| Alimony paid by the parents | $16,264,47 | |
| Alimoney supplementation through A.D.C. | | $67,817.00 |
| Alimony supplementation thru welfare | | 9,806.24 |
| | Total | $77,623,24 |

($77,623.24 per month means about $931,478.00 per year in Oakland County, or $10 million a year in the state).

## PART IV

# CRIMINAL JUSTICE NEEDS CIVIL PROCEDURES AND SOCIAL SERVICES

## Chapter XXXI

## PRESENT CRIMINAL PROCEDURE

Our Criminal Law excludes all social services until conviction has occurred.

Presently, in our free society, all persons, including the indicted or accused, are presumed innocent and are constitutionally protected against self incrimination. The Constitution also prevents arrest without probable cause, prohibits interrogated admissions or confessions unless clearly voluntary and protects against search of one's person or dwelling unless by search warrant or incidental to a proper arrest, namely, to find fruits of the crime or for arrest safety.

The person charged is encompassed by a continuing presumption of innocense, entitled to a fair trial, by jury or court as he chooses, to be represented by attorney at public expense if necessary and to be confronted by all witnesses who may be thoroughly cross examined. Violation of any of his rights may result in his acquittal.

So it is that we, the innocent, are afforded all these protective rights. So too, the guilty receive and may profit by these same protections.

The results are twofold. First, no innocent person is endanged but Second, often the guilty go free because though guilty, he cannot or is not proven guilty by competent proof beyond a reasonable doubt.

Now this protective framework necessarily causes certain procedures to be adopted by both the prosecution and the defense counsel. These exclude all the benefits of social services.

*Reductions of Charges—*

Often the prosecution is unable to clearly establish guilt beyond reasonable doubt. In such case he rests on the horns of a dilemma;

shall he run his chances of failure by jury acquittal of a respondent believed, but not clearly provable, guilty? Or shall he compromise with the respondent's attorney by adding a second count and allowing the defendant to plead guilty, as a compromise, to such lessor or included offense? For instance, a weak case of armed robbery, carrying a maximum of imprisonment of life may, with the prosecutor's approval, be compromised by allowing defendant to plead to a lesser or included offense such as robbery unarmed which carries a maximum of 15 years, or to felonious assault bearing 4 years, or a lesser offense involving probation. The result is a false concept of justice and a false criminal record. On the other hand, if the character of the respondent could be analyzed before plea, these legal gymnastics could usually be avoided. For instance, if a guilty defendant were to know and be assured of probable probation because of fair character, he would plead guilty to the true charge in most cases.

*Refusal of Cooperation—*

Take the matter of interrogation and cooperation. The capable defense counsel will probably instruct his client to remain absolutely uncommunicative and refuse all aid to law enforcement officers. Answer no questions whatsoever. This is wise, usually, for he has nothing to lose thereby and everything to gain. His silence cannot be used against him, whereas voluntary statements or cooperative assistance in solving the crime may result in confessions or admissions or evidence to his detriment. He may silently sit by, have the full benefit of all the facts shown at preliminary examination, and the testimony of accusing witnesses as well as technical inaccuracies of trial documents or defects in procedure, yet need not even take the witness stand himself. Thus the entire burden of proof beyond reasonable doubt rests with the prosecution. The guilty defendant rests silently on his legal rights, and is both uncommunicative and uncooperative.

*No Social Investigation—*

Under present legal strategy no social investigation, character diagnosis or planning of assistance can be had before trial. These services must await trial and conviction. Thus the benefits therefrom and credit for good facets of character cannot be measured and utilized before conviction. So many a guilty respondent who really merits probation or camp training and education must be first convicted by full scale trial wherein he is falsely painted innocent. Whereas confession would serve both his own moral good and society as well, much better. Attorneys could well learn to offer their clients to probation pre-sentence investigation on a privileged communication basis before trial. Often trial would then be unnecessary.

# CHAPTER XXXII

# NEW, MODERN JUSTICE DEMANDS
# SOCIAL-LEGAL PROGRESS

For many years criminal justice has made little social progress, except in the Juvenile Court. It has acted legalistically without benefit of skilled social services. Firmly established legal principles have satisfied the knowledgeable lawyers.

The occasional cries for reform have been faint. Offenders enduring useless punishments, thinking professors urging corrective legislation, these have generally gone unheeded. A few news stories challenging the archaic penal system have been overwhelmed by scandalous or spectacular crime news. Only a few of the more sensational criminal trials are publicized. Dope peddling, prostitution and disorderly conduct; these common matters of antisocial misbehavior, are so taken for granted as to be unnewsworthy, absent a name-bearing respondent. So most crime goes unreported.

Hence, the sad plight of the vast number of families of criminals is entirely ignored by the press. The public does not know about them. So the criminal courts grind on and on, generally without public attention or social concern. The repetitious misdemeanant and his ruined family are simply considered not newsworthy. Even though these constitute the bulk of our crime problem. Even though these are the embryo felons. Even though intelligence demands our attention.

But others like the sit-down, lay-down peace disturber who is a publicity seeker and who violates law and order primarily for self aggrandizement and at most, only secondarily serves a dubious social cause—all these receive extended press report.

So the real social spoilers, the repeated misdemeanant, the social recidivist, the family destroyer, these pass through the courts unheralded and unnoticed by the general public.

Recorder's Court processes thousands of unreported cases each year. What does society and its courts do to correct this flow of social destruction? Except for excellent probation in many cases, and good training camp programs for older felony offenders, we punish them by incarceration and then wash our hands of them. We hide ostrich like, from the true cause and effect of their misbehavior. We fail to see them as the fruit of our careless disinterest.

Never has society been so well off, yet with so many contagious miscreants of its own disinterested creation.

Poverty of the soul is ignored. Our churches which are morally interested are socially irresponsive. Because these good church members are sheltered and without social knowledge or challenge. We worship zealously, yet clear our minds of the plight of our unfortunate fellowmen. We need, therefore, a renaissance of social-criminal concept. A return, not via communistic prattle, but to our own Christian beliefs. Facing our responsibility to fellowmen, those less fortunate. Those who otherwise tend to despoil the beauty of today's American life. We need to revise our criminal-social process and procedure.

Judicially we must recede from the doctrine "Let the Punishment Fit the Crime". Socially, we must discard the theory that "education makes morality" and the assertion that "civil rights make good citizens". Even the semi-truth that "living standards make morality", is a weak palliative.

These are all misleading false doctrines or half truths.

In their place we must establish a new public concept, that—

*Criminal procedure must be non-punative, and to aid the offender as well as protect the public.*

It must be modernized as a social-legal progressive step forward. If we keep this purpose in mind, we will produce a reformation. But only by drastic revision and the use of skilled social services.

# Chapter XXXIII

# OUR "ONE COURT OF JUSTICE"— NEEDS SERVICES

The "One Court of Justice" of Michigan is seriously handicapped from crime deterrence because:

(1) It lacks state corrective training camps, and

(2) It lacks skilled probationary and social services, and usually

(3) Lacks community assistance.

Nearly every dangerous felon began his misbehavior in minor misdemeanors. Circuit court records so attest. Poor citizenship, accented by multiple anti-social misdemeanors. The drunk, the disorderly person, the minor assaulter, the petty thief, the non-supporter, the child neglector; these are misdemeanants.

They are charged with misdemeanor complaint and arraigned before the various municipal or justice courts. These judges, with rare exception, as in Detroit's overburdened Recorders Court, have no skilled probation services available, no use of psychologists, social case workers or psychiatrists, and usually no way of diagnosing or serving the many personal and family problems involved.

There are no work-education camps, no corrective homes and no other corrective custodial facilities available for misdemeanor violators, even though teenagers. We have no Youth Authority Act. These offenders cannot be given custodial care other than jail incarceration unless and until they have committed felonies. Further, community resources such as Alcoholic Anonymous, mental guidance clinics, family service agencies and church social services are either unavailable or unused for the most part. Thus most repeater and recidivistic misdemeanants are:

(1) simply fined, or

(2) placed in the county jail for 90 days or less, or

(3) placed on probation without any skilled supervision or social services.

Further, those who need to be under custodial training programs for correction cannot be so cared for as misdemeanor violators. Ironically they must await conviction as felons before they may be admitted to a state work-education training camp. (See Michigan Statutes Annotated 28.1134 and 28.1683).

When the fairly good citizen commits a misdemeanor offense, the threat of jail is in itself sufficient corrective medicine. On the other hand, the anti-social or recidivistic or socially inadequate citizen finds the threat of jail or its consummation little feared. The sad fact is that repetitious misdemeanor mishehavior increases the community rejection of the misdemeanant. His family thereby becomes even more socially depressed and rejected. The ultimate result under our obsolete criminal system of punishment by fine or jail, is that we create felons out of our failure with misdemeanants.

Nearly all poverty of today results from personal inadequacy, whether educationally or otherwise, and from plain poor citizenship. Thus, if we are to use Federal poverty money wisely, we would do well to siphon considerable of it into projects which would prevent crime. This can best be done by improving the character of the misdemeanor respondents and their family.

To serve their purpose, the Michigan misdemeanor courts must be given adequate—

(1) Skilled probation and social services;

(2) State correctional camps; and

(3) Community assistance.

# CHAPTER XXXIV

# JUDICIAL EFFICIENCY DEMANDS ADMINISTRATIVE SERVICES

The good Juvenile Court protects all constitutional and human rights of children and families. But it goes far beyond this by full use of skilled social services. With the acknowledged purpose to help children, rather than to punish, most children and parents are cooperative. Knowing the court will not be punitive but will assist the child at fault or in trouble, they answer questions willingly. Constitutional rights are thus not invaded. No portion of the adversary system is abandoned.

Thus in 95 percent of the cases the basic facts are soon acknowledged. The truth, so necessary for justice, usually is ascertained with little or no adversary trial. In the remaining 5 percent, this same work of the skilled professionals is most useful to the lawyers involved. In exercising the adversary function they have scientific study and evaluation to work with.

In the absence of lawyers, the court makes like use thereof. Interrogation is informal, but still observes evidentiary rules. So the Juvenile Court has not abandoned the adversary system. Instead it has improved upon criminal court procedure, so that the lawyers need not depend entirely thereon.

But actually this step toward efficiency in judicial procedure by the use of skilled services, is taking place in many other fields of the law.

For instance, pretrial deposition, interrogatories and discovery is the use of investigatory legal skills without adversary trial surprise and tricky interrogation at trial. Thoroughness in these preliminary activities is comparable to the thorough use of social professional skills. It vastly reduces the basis and need for contested adversary trials.

Many facts are now agreed upon and stiplated to. In negligence cases virtually the entire reports of medical witnesses may be fully known to all parties long before trial and even stipulated to as established facts.

In another sense preliminary examination in felony cases also lays most of the facts bare, thereby avoiding much of the controversial adversary contest.

Again, careful and thorough social investigation in divorce cases will not only eliminate much of the adversary conflict but will also treat the unfortunate children in a much more kindly fashion.

Thus I believe the trend throughout the law is to use all professional skills much more extensively in scientifically ascertaining the truth. The lawyer is far better off to aid the realization of truth. The modern attorney may well use the adversary proceedings as a legal skill, valuable over and beyond the scientifically ascertainable truths. But even here, the adversary system is valuable in total social justice when limitedly used. Namely, only in proving his meritorious client is really deserving. Never in thwarting justice. Never by distorting the true image of guilt or innocence. Never by confusing merit with lack of cause.

Thus most civil justice injects modern scientific procedures, facilities and skills into our judicial systems to further the efficiency of our existing adversary system. But criminal justice has made no such progress. It is still in its antiquated technical state.

When human behavior is involved, these new professional skills of social investigation, psychology, counselling, pediatrics and psychiatry are tools to be used by the lawyer and court alike. Tools which are now basic necessities to the ultimate ends of justice.

Thus the well established trends in Juvenile Court, Circuit Court pretrials, and controversies, negligence cases, auto insurance matters and divorce and family law cases, are all pointed to the increased use of scientific services; and the consequent lessening of the use of the old fashioned adversary system.

Adversary contest is still the cornerstone of the judicial system. But is is now greatly enlightened by available skilled services. Criminal Courts must learn how to use the social sciences in aid of criminal justice. This requires social-legal revision and modernization of criminal practice and procedure.

# CHAPTER XXXV

# OUR CRIMINAL PROCEDURE
# NEEDS REVISION

The recent United States Supreme Court decisions on arrest, search and seizure, confessions, self incrimination, presumption of innocence, counsel for indigents and trial procedure, are not new criminal law. Basically, they are restatements of old established principles. They are obviously just and necessary protections for the innocent in our free society.

But on the other hand the general public has become more and more at the mercy of and without protection from the many criminals at large. These never had it so good. They are close to being a protected class for whom the technical law innocently discriminates. Crime is increasing. Everyone is endangered. As a matter of protection of the general public, we must immediately find a solution. And it must be within our constitutional safeguards.

Police work now requires extensive education for the intricacies of the now more difficult duties. Thus, our police officers must soon have several years of advanced police education and training. They must be paid commensurate with college graduates.

This will be all right, in the long run, if we may somehow still adequately protect the general public from crime. But crime is now so easy to perpetrate, so difficult to prevent, and so far out of hand. Even with more highly trained and skillful police officers, under present law we may lose the battle against crime.

It is a lawyer's duty to represent his client. Protection "beyond reasonable doubt", has been greatly fortified and strengthened by the newly restated Supreme Court decisions. These Supreme Court decisions give every miscreant a lawyer and afford more protections for the accused. Soon every misdemeanant, such as the common thief, will have a lawyer furnished; and more legal safeguards. We may even be economically unable to prosecute. More often we shall be unable to convict.

Let me illustrate. The petty thief, unless caught red-handed in the act, and proven guilty by eye witnesses, will now probably go free. For several reasons. Suppose he acts furtively and is seen running a block from the scene of the theft. A police officer or citizen cannot legally apprehend and arrest him. The reason is simple. A warrant is first needed. Since the stolen articles are of less than $100 value, the offense amounts only to a misdemeanor violation. An arrest and search without warrant, for a misdemeanor offense not committed in the officer's presence is illegal.

The thief also knows he need not answer questions. Further, only if he is legally arrested when apprehended, may he be searched for fruits of the crime, namely, the stolen articles. Likewise he may be searched for weapons only when such search is a part of the safety precautions of a valid arrest. If a concealed weapon is found on him, or the stolen articles, the arrest and search may both be held unwarranted. The stolen goods and the concealed weapon may both be suppressed from evidence as the product of an illegal arrest and search.

Think of some of the other roadblocks to police work. The wise crook will now refuse to go to police headquarters for interrogation. For he now knows he need not answer a single question. And if he is arrested he may insist on an attorney. If he is indigent, an attorney must immediately be furnished. The attorney will remind him to say nothing, insist on his being taken immediately before the nearest judge and released forthwith on reasonable bond. Gone is the police fort of interrogation, to plead for the truth, the custom of taking him to the scene of the crime. Even the right to bring witnesses to identify him may be lost unless done very promptly.

Further, pause must be had to determine whether his prosecution is worth the expense involved. Worst of all, even after trial and fair conviction he may burden the public with large expense of unmeritorious appeals to which he has a constitutional right though without any probable cause for appeal.

These facts illustrate the plight of the unprotected public. Merely by our courts affording us our desired constitution safeguards, these same protections have now become an unconscionable shield for the guilty.

Thus, we must change and revise our criminal procedure in order to adequately protect the public. I suggest we may well do this and yet remain within constitutional criminal law. Solution is available as follows:

Two changes are necessary—

(1) *As to Felonies of Wilful Violence—*

We must make indeterminate prison sentence mandatory in all wilful and violence criminal felonies. For life or until re-respondents prove themselves so improved in characters as to reasonably reliable on parole. This will remove more permanently many dangerous criminals.

(2) *As to Misdemeanors—*
We must provide two optional civil procedures; namely, First, the alternative option to provide monetary civil action penalties for non-repetitive misdemeanors.
Second, corrective guardianship over socially inadequate persons designed primarily for the benefit and welfare of the respondents as social deviates.

These civil statutes will not require constitutional amendment. They will be alternative to criminal action. They will be non-punitive, and non-criminal, civil in nature. They will resemble the guardianship assistance, protection and treatment afforded by mental illness guardianship and hospitalization in present Probate Court practice. They may follow the civil procedure of the modern Juvenile Court. They will provide treatment instead of punishment. This follows our modern concepts of social fairness and assistance.

The writer has learned through some 25 years of experience that the Juvenile Court law of assistance to children is the pattern to follow in reforms of criminal law. We must furnish assistance to the accused and protection to the public. This means simply that we adopt two basic concepts universally followed by Juvenile Courts:

*First*—That we have a duty to strive to change the immoral character of the law violator, and to segregate him in curative or guardianship custody until he is likely to be law abiding.

*Second*—That the court serves the public better in aiding the respondent instead of only punishing him. Substitute insistent assistance in place of punitive imprisonment. Such services as probation, psychiatric care, psychological counselling, education, moral training and community acceptance, are needed. These should be afforded in the place of the public degradation, stigmatization, imprisonment and resultant recidivism which now accompany our criminal process. Most of all we need work-education camps for these misdemeanants, who are embryo felons, where they may learn to work instead of sitting idly by in jail.

To effect these advances, we must first modify certain antiquated legal doctrines. We must approach crime prevention scientifically.

There are two basically different classes of law violators—
*First,* Those fairly socially responsible who will not run away.

105

Their community roots of ownership, home and family, and local attachments compel them to remain and face the charges. They are fair citizens, capable of reformation. Civil penalty will here serve better than criminal incarceration. With these, skillful probation is 95 percent successful.

*Second,* on the other hand, there are those who are very likely to abscond, and commit other crimes because they are repeaters. They have no ties to hold them. They are either repetitive recidivists or those given to anti-social living. They belong in curative custody such as training camps.

The dividing line is not always clear cut, but most respondents fall rather definitely into one class or the other. If a respondent is willing to cooperate, a rapid police investigation can promptly classify respondents either as potential absconders of unreliable propensities or reasonably trustworthy and responsible by civil summons to civil court process.

Having so determined it is important to carefully separate out the criminals who are very dangerous to society. They commit crimes of violence like murder, rape by force, felonious assault, armed robbery, kidnapping and the like. They must be criminally prosecuted and sent to prison under indeterminate sentence. There are other less dangerous persons who are repetitive recidivists, like the drunkard, the sex offender, the drug addict, the common thief or the prostitute. They need social treatment, either civil or criminal.

Those who are dangerous to society have no community roots or loyalty, are absconders and are amenable to little reformatory assistance. They must be prosecuted as criminals. On conviction they should never be afforded probation. Instead they must be securely confined in treatment centers for criminals. Their indeterminate sentences should be for from one year to life imprisonment. They should all remain in such custody indefinitely, until after treatment, their personality and character is demonstratively changed and improved to warrant parole.

Civil procedure, instead of criminal procedure for lesser offenses will not deny a respondent any constitutional rights. Rather it will often afford him a right to avoid criminal record; and to show by fair disclosure that he should be treated as a civil, non-criminal law violator.

This would work as follows: Suppose a person is about to be arrested for disorderly conduct or simple larceny committed in the officer's presence.

Before arrest a polite but careful interrogation can easily be had to learn his identity, residence, employment and similar information tending to show his quality of citizenship.

If it appears he has substantive and credible character, a civil summons could well be issued. This civil summons would be authorized by law, and be very similar to the customary traffic violation ticket.

Before the hearing date a cursory social investigation of respondent's character may be summarily made. His job, work record, family situation and past record of misconduct can easily be ascertained.

If he is of good general character without serious or repetitive criminal record, his civil trial or admission of misbehavior will result in a fine, or fine and probation. Incarceration would be unnecessary.

As to the law violations which are not recidivistic and not of wilful violence they must be thought of, pursued and treated in an entirely new, different fashion. Namely, as treatment for the benefit of the individual. A civil procedure for his welfare. Like hospitalization for the mentally ill, or enforced medical treatment for tuberculosis. Or guardianship for the mentally inadequate. Here it will be guardianship for a socially inadequate person.

The benefits will be immeasurable. Let us consider them.

First, most misdemeanor violators, namely lesser offenders may be charged in civil rather than criminal proceedings. Being civil in nature, the respondent will then be brought before the court by summons rather than arrest. If he denies the violation he may be interrogated without violating any constitutional privilege. He may be required to testify even against his will, as in any other civil case.

Since the offense will not be a crime, he may not be imprisoned therefor. However, he may be fined and be subject to contempt procedings, if, being able, he still refused to pay the fine.

Consider the violator needing corrective treatment. This being a civil procedure designed for his moral and social welfare, for his own protection, a thorough social investigation may be had. If the investigation shows needs for his moral and social welfare, the court may place him under probationary or guardianship supervision to that end and order him to comply with such suitable conditions, and even with custodial care and treatment.

Take the case of an alcoholic. He is picked up by police protectively for drunk and disorderly conduct. On immediately learning, by taking him home, that he is not a floater, migrant or non-resident, he may be given over to the custody of his family. If he is not a repetitious criminal, a civil complaint may be filed against him and he may be given a summons to appear in court at a day and time certain.

107

If he is socially inadequate, a repeated violator or of seriously immoral character, a social investigation should immediately be set in motion. A great deal should be promtply learned about his personality, previous record and personal family needs. Does he hold a job? Support his family? Often misbehave? Repeatedly become intoxicated? Own his home or have assets? In short, such preliminary investigation would show him in his true light as a fair, bad or inadequate citizen. This is the essence of modern municipal court procedure like that of Judge Leenhouts of Royal Oak Municipal Court.

On the trial date these investigation facts may be confirmed or disproved. If he is a "first time" drunk without prior offense he may be fined civilly, admonished and no supervision may be necessary.

On the other hand, if he is a confirmed alcoholic and his family and he are both being injured, he may be ordered under medical treatment, psychiatric or psychological counselling, hospitalization if necessary and close supervision afforded. In subsequent supervision further investigation could be had and his behavior would come to light and additional deficiencies and needs could be administered to.

Take the sex misbehavior case where violence is not involved, such as indecent exposure, or indecent liberties, or solicitation. These are psychiatric cases.

In the absence of wilful violence, only one basic matter is involved; namely, corrective treatment through psychiatry and psychology, for only thus may the public be protected and the respondent assisted. Here again, hospitalization on an indeterminate basis could likewise be ordered in severe cases as a civil remedy to aid the individual involved as well as to protect society.

Take traffic violations. The only real protection the public has against the careless, negligent driver is to get him off the road by loss of license and civil contempt for violation of a court order directing him not to drive.

In most negligent homicide cases, imprisonment of the respondent serves no useful purpose. Fear as a deterient is seldom involved. Careful driving is an attitude of mind coupled with a skill of driving. Injury when inflicted is instantaneous. Too late then, to be in fear of imprisonment. It would be much better indeed to order restitution and payment of bills incurred, revoke drivers' licenses and explore the character of the wrongdoer. Attention to his general behavior with a corrective purpose would do far more towards reducing future injury to the public.

Lastly, think generally of present criminal law. We usually imprison respondents simply as punishment because we know no better course.

Perhaps this satisfies our animal nature as vengeance. Actually we are hiding our heads in the sand, willing to hope fear and punishment will serve society instead of affirmative, constructive, social and medical treatment. These skills are available. Why not use them?

Pre-sentence investigations of those to be sent to state prisons show case histories with one basic, fundamental fact. The felon of today is the product of our ignoring the prior misdemeanor offenses of the same respondent. These reports always show repeated prior misdemeanors, of drunkenness, disorderly conduct, careless car driving, petty thievery, non-support and similar misbehavior. No wonder indeed that these habits of bad citizenship blossom into felonies of violence. If we believe children need corrective treatment, why fool ourselves that adults are different? If adults without social assistance have proven themselves incapable of self correction, why rely on outmoded penal imprisonment?

Or lastly, since treatment of juvenile offenders has proven worth its weight in gold, why not resort to the social medicine of treatment of adults instead of punishment?

In all of this we search for progress. We shall make no real social progress merely by extending our criminal technicalities to misdemeanor cases, as the Supreme Court has required. Shall the drunkard, the disorderly person, the reckless driver, the wife non-supporter, the socially irresponsible bum and panhandler, shall these now all be afforded their technical constitutional rights but given no social assistance and controls? Presumption of innocence, immunity from self incrimination, jury trial, lawyers at public expense and appeals at will are important. But shall we flounder into deeper public expense without gainful purpose? Shall we become economically immersed in legalistic maize? Or shall we use modern skills to reduce embryo crime? By social assistance and control?

Let us go about helping the criminal who is capable of improvement. Let us use civil cure procedure. Let us avoid the cumbersome penalistic criminal procedure. Let us put away more permanently by indeterminate sentence, the wilful and violent offenders and the repetitive recidivists who are incurable.

In short let us retain all the good protections of criminal law. But let us progress through the use of civil procedures and skilled social services.

This indeed, will be New Justice for all!

*1965 Graduates of Girls' Ranch and Boys' Ranch, successfully going on to college*

111

# HUNG OVER, SLEEP-DEPRIVED, OVER-CAFFEINATED, AND LIVING ON PIZZA

*Is This the Only Way to Get Through College?*
*Success Tips for a Healthier Four Years*

KATHY *Parry*

Your Real Food Coach

# Hung Over, Sleep-Deprived, Over-Caffeinated, and Living on Pizza

## A Kathy Parry Book

Book Cover by Tracey Miller | www.TraceOfStyle.com
Publishing by Weston Lyon | www.WestonLyon.com
Edited by Lauren Cullumber

ISBN:1499179219
EAN-13: 978-1499179217

**Disclaimer:**
This book contains opinions, ideas and experiences and is not intended as medical and/or health advice. Please consult a medical professional before adopting any of the suggestions in this book.

**For My Kids: Paige, JP and Graham**

You're almost never stupid and I'm so proud of you. Thank you for your love and support. And sorry we never had Twinkies in the house.

Love you!

# Hung Over, Sleep-Deprived, Over-Caffeinated, and Living on Pizza

## Table of Contents

Read This First ....................................................... 7

Chapter 1: Hung Over ............................................. 11

Chapter 2: Sleep-Deprived ..................................... 27

Chapter 3: Over-Caffeinated ................................... 43

Chapter 4: Living on Pizza ...................................... 57

Are You Done With Stupid? .................................... 77

Bonus Chapter: Stay Away ..................................... 79
from the Health Center

About the Author .................................................. 89

Stop Stupid on Your Campus! ................................ 93

The Ultimate Recipe for an Energetic Life .............. 95

# READ THIS FIRST!

"Dear God Girl, Pull Yourself Together"

I had the pleasure of spending five hours in the car driving my daughter and two friends back to college after semester break. These three had been at home for six weeks. Six weeks is a long time to go without parties and bars and late-night food bingeing. Their break had instead been consumed with crappy retail jobs, parental curfews and visits with great-aunts. But in the confined space of the car, with the anticipation of the return to fun, the stories started to flow.   Bridget, the most animated of the three, began telling a story of a sorority date party:

"So we were taking a bus to the party. And I did NOT pre-game with everyone. So I was not drunk at ALL getting on the bus. But you would not believe this girl sitting behind me. She obviously did pre-game, she was like already pretty drunk. And I do NOT know what happened, but she started slapping her date, standing up yelling. Her hands were waving. She was falling over. She was a mess!! I just wanted to turn around and say, 'Dear God Girl, Pull Yourself Together!'"

I laughed so hard I almost drove out of my lane into a passing semi-truck! At that moment I told Bridget,

"I do believe that should be the motto of every late night, over-indulged college student."

I'm a mom who doesn't freak out. Having four kids in seven years mellows you a bit. There just isn't time to get worked up about stuff. And on top of that, I've always been very open with my kids.

"Mom, did you ever drink beer in high school?" I was asked over dinner when my oldest was entering high school. I wasn't about to lie. I don't lie. "Yes, I did drink a little in high school," I answered. "But I wasn't stupid."

I hate stupid. Stupid gets college students in trouble. Stupid gets adults into trouble. Everyone likes to have fun. But when we cross the line into stupid, bad stuff happens. Embarrassing stuff happens. Laws get broken. You forget to sleep in your bed. You get sick. Stupid isn't good.

This book is about not being stupid. While riding in the car with my three college friends, I asked them, "What do you think are the biggest health problems facing college kids?" Immediately, without hesitation my daughter said, "Everyone is hung-over, sleep-deprived, over-caffeinated and eating bad."

"Oh my gosh! Text that to me," I pleaded as I drove. That was it. I'm a food coach and nutritional instructor, but it's been a few years since I've been in college. But her summary of the lifestyle brought it all flooding back.

I remember living on Wendy's® Chili and bagels for an entire winter when I lived off-campus. Fruit? Don't think so. Vegetables? Well, maybe a few carrots or the salad bar at Wendy's if I was feeling guilty. And the beer. Yes, lots of beer. My freshman RA used to say, "Beer is food." Technically yes, but nutritionally, not really. But we didn't care. We were stupid. My roommate carried a bar stool out of a bar one night and was chased down the street by the bouncer. Stupid. A friend showed up still drunk from the night before for her job at the rec center. She was fired. Stupid. We've all been stupid.

This book is not about alcohol education. If you're a college student, you've had that one crammed down your throat before you even graced the halls of your institute of higher learning. And you probably still got drunk and embarrassed yourself.

And this book is not a guide to a food pyramid. You saw the food pyramid and versions of a plate of healthful food all through your schooling. And you probably still ate pizza, mac n' cheese and Red Bull® until you felt sick or gained your freshman fifteen.

And this isn't a book about healthy sleep habits. You have a mother. She's been telling you to get your sleep for years, and you still don't.

This is a book about not being stupid. It is about balance. You will learn tips and tactics for moving through feeling bad after a night of drinking. You will begin to see the importance of nutrients. The stuff that your body needs, so when you reach your twenties you're not always catching colds or worse, a disease. You'll learn why caffeine only works temporarily and that unless you want to feel and look old before your time, you do have to sleep.

You can continue down the path of crappy lifestyle choices, but eventually to be successful, healthy, and energetic you will need to tell yourself, "Dear God, Pull Yourself Together!"

# Chapter 1

# **Hung Over**

## **One time when I was hung over:**

*"...I literally stayed in bed all day with friends circling in and out visiting. My friends still joke about visiting me at my death bed..."*

## The Moment of Truth

The morning after. You are in bed. Maybe your bed, but maybe you wake up in the bed of a friend across campus, a random frat house, of an unknown stranger. You're lying vertical and before you open your eyes you know what has happened. That last round of tequila shots has settled firmly in your head. As you attempt to open your eyes, the light that yesterday seemed so normal is now your nemesis. You're quite certain if you open your eyes, you will be blinded. Your head is pounding. Your stomach is queasy. And everything smells bad. You are hung over.

Maybe you were stupid and don't remember what happened. Check your surroundings. Are your clothes on? Do you have your ID and wallet? Is the person next to you someone whose name you know? Once you've established that all your important parts are ok, what do you do next? (Sneaking out of the room of the unknown stranger may be first...but then...) What is happening in your body and how can you fix it? You look at the clock, class starts in thirty minutes. Time to feel better quick.

## What Is A Hangover?

A hangover is being stupid. You drank more alcohol than your body could safely process. You may do some stupid things in college but it is best to learn from them and move on. Hanging your head over a toilet and feeling like a small animal is running around in your stomach is a good way to learn how your body reacts to alcohol, and may encourage you to prevent it from happening again.

A hangover is basically dehydration. Your body goes through a lot to process the alcohol. But the major player in the hangover game is water. Your headache comes as a result of your body taking water away from the brain to run other systems. This lack of water can also cause the swaying motion you experience as you try to put your feet on the floor. And as you dizzily try to make your way to the bottle of water sitting on your desk, you may be struck by a sudden queasiness in your stomach and lower intestines. The alcohol hitting your stomach causes inflammation and all kinds of digestive woes.

## Get To Know Your Liver

This could be a chapter about how alcohol works in your body. But why? That's what all standardized alcohol education is about. But in the bar at 1:00 AM all the online Alcohol Ed classes in the world aren't going to tell you anything you don't know: You drank too much. You got drunk. And now you're hungover. The part I want you to know is how to recover from it and how to avoid it next time. And to do that, you need to get to know your liver. You need to take care of your liver. Yes, lots of organs are affected by drinking too much. But if you want to recover and feel well, you better respect your liver.

The liver is like your annoying, over-involved friend. You know the one. She's on student government, belongs to a few save-the-planet organizations, takes 18 hours each semester and works with special-needs children on the weekends. She's a do-gooder and so nice no one can dislike her. That is your liver. The over-involved organ that only wants to do good.

Your liver fills its busy days with the following activities: processing nutrients from food, storing sugar to use for energy later, helping to make bile to digest fat, filtering all the chemicals you ingest, cleaning out bacteria, helping with blood clotting and most importantly to you on Saturday night, it processes alcohol.

After the beer...rum...Jagermeister®...has entered your bloodstream it remains in your body until it is processed. And the average person can process about one drink an hour. Oops...did you just have five? You've just created an emergency situation in your liver. Your body becomes a detox factory. A giant Brita filter. Between 90-98% of the alcohol you guzzled down is

**15**

broken down in your liver. The other 2-10% of the alcohol comes out when you pee, sweat or breathe. Morning breath on any college campus could be 2-10% alcohol! But when you over-indulge, your liver can't keep up. Nights and nights of this treatment and your liver will become taxed and inefficient. And if your liver is busy with all this detox stuff, just look at the list above to realize what it **isn't** doing. Too much detox work, not enough time to digest well, not enough time to build energy stores, not enough time to help you stay healthy.

So if you want to process the alcohol in the most efficient manner, get through the hangover quickly and feel better, you're going to have to show your liver some love. You're going to have to show all of you some love. And not in the "I will feel better if I do a little online shopping" type of love. Or "if I go find an easy hook up I'll feel better about myself" situation. If you want your body to feel well, you're going to have to show it a little respect.

Below are some tips to move you through a hangover and some tactics for drinking that won't land you in the hospital ER with the campus police on a phone call home to the parents, while you fade in and out of consciousness. That is stupid.

# Tips For Dealing With A Hangover

## Tip #1:

Water Before, Water During, Water After

Part of the college experience is to get wasted. But getting drunk isn't the optimal way to treat your body. (And if you're underage...it's illegal...just saying). But if you're not ready to be part of the milk and cookies club, you'll need to learn your limits and take a few steps to avoid the hangover.

Learning your limits is a bit like the fifth grade science experiment when one half of the class put their sunflower seeds in sunlight and the other half didn't. Everyone knows the sunlight half grew taller flowers. Everyone knows if you don't drink you don't get hung over. But if you want to drink you have to honor the scientific process and pay attention to the variables.

The biggest variable in the hangover experiment is water. Because alcohol dehydrates the body you need to be in the control group that adds water. Your head aches the next day because your brain is lacking water. **You must drink water before you start to drink alcohol.** When you start drinking in a hydrated state, your body starts processing from a good state. Your tank is full instead of empty.

You need to continue to honor hydration during the next stage of your evening, a party with trashcans filled with Jungle Juice. When you dip into the can of Jungle Juice you also need to grab a water bottle.

Say you're drinking at a house party and you don't know how to get a bottle of water. This is a perfect time to make a new friend. Ask around. There is a case of water bottles sitting somewhere. Don't be shy about asking for water at a bar. Every time you order a pitcher of beer, order a pitcher of water. **Have a plan for drinking water all night**.

---

## One time when I was hung over:

*"...I wore see-through leggings and bright blue underwear to meet with my professor to discuss my research paper..."*

---

But if you forgot about water and you wake up feeling like the sunflower shriveling up in the desert, then start hydrating immediately. Your stomach may feel queasy, but drink water anyway. The very best type of water you can drink is water with lemon juice in it.

Quick, send your roommate to the dining hall or Chipotle® and grab some lemons. Lemons are one of the few foods that help the liver produce extra enzymes. And liver enzymes help process the alcohol and detox your body. Continue to drink water all day. All day.


## Tip #2:
Ready...Set...Drink. No, Eat.

You think you're ready to drink. The music has been cranking. Econ notes are taken. Your buddy is texting that the scene at your favorite club is looking good. But the last thing you ate was cheese crackers from a vending machine. No worries, you'll grab something while you're out.

Stop. Just stop. You need to eat. This is not your grandma telling you to eat because she's afraid you won't grow. This is the voice of science and reason telling you to fill your stomach with some food before the alcohol.

Food slows the absorption of alcohol. So yes, you may not get the buzz on as fast, but you also won't feel as crappy in the morning. The best foods to eat before drinking involve some fat. One of the very best pre-game foods are eggs.

Maybe "Kegs and Eggs" is the most healthful party of the year? But eggs have an amino acid called cycsteine that helps break down the toxins in alcohol. Does your campus bagel shop have an egg salad sandwich? Can you stop off at the dining hall with an omelet option? If you can't find an egg, look for some healthful fatty foods. Eating good fats found in foods like guacamole or hummus is way better for the hangover than a bunch of wings.

## Tip #3:
## Good Night, Sleep Tight: Before Bed Tactics

I got drunk one night and my friend Pam tried to help me out. She stood in front of my dresser and said, "You need to put on some pajamas. Which ones do you want?" as she held up a pink pair and a yellow pair. "I want the purple ones," I said as I pointed to the yellow. She shook her head and helped me into the pajamas. I hope you have a few nice friends like that, the ones who look after you when you're a bit stupid. Pam wanted to help. And she did. But besides making sure you don't wake up in your clothes, there are a few other tactics that are helpful before you go to bed.

First, you're going to come home drunk, so you need to make a plan before you get drunk. Because drunk-people plans usually involve stealing crap and knocking on the door of your crush or the University President. Making a bedtime plan before you get drunk works almost as well as purple pajamas.

Before you go out, set a water bottle or two beside your bed. When you see it, you may even remember to drink it before you crawl under the covers. But if you don't drink it while in your inebriated state, at least you'll see it in the morning. Next to that you may want to set out some ibuprofen (Motrin®). **You do not want to take** Acetaminophen (Tylenol®) **because it is processed through your liver.** And remember, your liver is a little busy right now. But a better thing to set out is a banana on your bedside table. You will lose potassium during a night of drinking. Eating a banana before bed will reduce the chances of a hangover the next morning. And make sure your phone is next to your bed, in case you need to call a friend like Pam to help you out.

## Tip #4:

The Moment of Truth...Good Morning

My friend Todd told me a story about waking up in college after a big night of drinking. His first sensation was that of a weight on top of his chest. His eyes were still glued shut by the effects of the keg, but the smell and heaviness on his chest made him realize the weight

**21**

was a person. His first thought was, "please don't let her be ugly" and his second thought, "please let it be a her."

The morning after is the moment of truth. Will you be able to move in the manner of a human or will you be more sloth-like today? If you drank more alcohol than your body could process, did not drink water all night with your alcohol, did not eat food before you drank...you get the picture...you may have earned yourself a hangover. What's next?

"...Combos® and Gatorade®...."

"...More alcohol and McDonald's® breakfast..."

"...Lying in bed longer and then making a super greasy breakfast to soak up the rest of the alcohol..."

# One time when I was hung over:

*"...I got sick 5 times during the day until 6 pm the next evening :( I had to keep running out of my classes and it was awful..."*

Every college student has their list. Greasy food seems to be on top. But it doesn't really soak up the alcohol. For some people the fat calms their stomach, but it isn't the most healthful way to recover. Instead you need to stick to foods that love your liver, help your detox systems, and replace what the alcohol has depleted.

A lot of people think Gatorade is a hangover cure-all, but it is loaded with sugar and artificial colors. Who hasn't heard, "You need to replace your electrolytes"? And because of some awesome marketing using millionaire athletes, we all think that means you need to guzzle artificially colored and flavored crap. Your liver actually has to detox those things away.

Electrolytes just refer to a handful of minerals that your body needs to carry electric charges throughout your body. When you become dehydrated, your mineral balance goes out of whack.

So what do you eat and drink the next day to help your head? Start out only with liquids for the first hour. You must rehydrate before you eat. Here's my hangover food and drink recovery list:

- Water with a pinch of sea salt for minerals and juice from half a lemon.

- Coconut water for the natural electrolytes and vitamins.

- Green juices for the vast nutrients and alkaline affect.

- Cucumbers for liver cleansing.

- Bananas for magnesium and potassium.

- Black Beans (Get up to Chipotle!) for magnesium.

- Spinach for phosphorus and its alkaline affect.

- Nuts for phosphorus.

- Complex carbs with small amount of protein after an hour or two.

- Avoid fatty foods. Your body just isn't ready to process them and they can make you feel worse.

# Stupid Stopped

Rachel was ready to go. It was Thursday night and her Friday classes didn't start until 11:00. She was so ready to party. Turning in her Art Theory project and finishing her Western Civ reading happened early today. So tonight was a guilt-free party night.

Her group of friends headed to a party at the fraternity house where her friends knew a lot of the guys. Rachel didn't go out with this group as often, but she was up for meeting some new people. Rachel and her friends hit the keg and started to dance. Only a few songs later Rachel realized she was feeling a buzz. But it was all good.

The group headed into one brother's room and vodka drinks were poured. Rachel took a sip and realized this drink was strong. Her head was starting to feel more and more fuzzy. She put the drink down and asked about some water. The guys laughed and poured her more to drink.

As the room became louder with her messed up friends, Rachel quietly slipped out of the room. She found her way to a quieter area and asked a guy who seemed kind of mellow if he knew where she could get some water. He led her to the kitchen and grabbed a water bottle.

Besides stopping a stupid night of excessive drinking, Rachel ended up talking to the guy a good part of the night.

# Chapter 2

# **Sleep-Deprived**

**The Stupidest Thing I Ever Did
Because I Was Sleep-Deprived:**

*"I fell asleep in class, a deep sleep. The professor
called my name multiple times before physically
shaking me to wake me up."*

# Good Night, Sleep Tight

The chairs on the first floor of the main library — that's where I'd find him. Paul always took his naps at the exact same spot. I needed his notes and it was certain that on most any given Wednesday at 4:00 in the afternoon, I could find him asleep in the orange chair. The public power nap. It is the way most students survive their schedules. All over college campuses, students seek out their spot. Some look for the chair that is the right size. Some look for a quiet spot. But if you're like most students, it really doesn't matter where your head falls. At some point it just hits the desk. You're out.

Late nights are just part of your life right now. Papers need to be written, groups need to be met with, parties get going and keep going and the next thing you know, you've forgotten about sleep. We only have so many hours in a day and when we need more hours we rob from the sleep bank. But like even the best-planned heist, someone usually gets caught. And when we rob from our sleep hours, we end up the loser in a jail cell with disease, weight gain, lousy immune function and let's not forget, a cranky attitude.

The whole sleep cycle dynamic at school is a bit like the Sponge Bob® episode when Sandy the squirrel is preparing for hibernation. Oh come on, you know you watched every episode at least a half dozen times. It isn't the one where she is already asleep and Patrick and Sponge Bob interrupt her dream, but the one when she's getting ready to sleep. Sponge Bob commits all his time to her for the week and they play every dangerous game a Texas squirrel with a high tolerance for pain can imagine. Games like "Find the Hay in the Needlestack" and "Extreme Jacks" ensue. (Sound just a bit like your life? "Find the Bottom of the Keg" and "Extreme Paper Writing"?) The games end up sending a beaten-up Sponge Bob into hiding. But Sandy, not wanting to miss out on any fun, continues on her mission of playing dangerous games, all the while hunting for Sponge Bob. When Sandy eventually finds Sponge Bob she tells him that they have just enough time to go "Atom Smashing" before she has to hibernate. But it's too late; Sandy has exhausted herself and falls sound asleep.

Bet you've felt like Sandy. Too much extreme fun. Too much extreme studying. And you crash.

## What's a Body Without Sleep?
## Sick, Dumb and Fat

About six weeks into the first semester, the Health and Wellness Centers across college campuses fill up. This is about how long it takes for a body to wear out from the extremes. Studies have shown that there are certain functions in the body that only happen when we sleep. Sleep becomes a time to repair and restore. In one study, animals were completely deprived of sleep and eventually died. A little severe for your life, but I bet some students feel that way at the end of Pledge Week or a grueling finals week. Cellular functions of healing and immune response happen when we aren't spending energy walking to class or dancing at a club. During the day your body is just too darn busy living the life to do the necessary repair work that needs to be done. No time for sleep = no time to heal.

And your body doesn't just get unhealthy without sleep; you also get stupid. In studies where subjects were allowed only four hours of sleep for four days, the impairments to their health and wellbeing began after only one sleep-deprived night. One of the first things to go is memory. This does not come as a shock to me. I once pulled an all-nighter before an Accounting final. I was so sleep-deprived and sketchy in my head after a night with no sleep that I sat confused and dazed while attempting to take the exam. Yes, my grade sucked. I still hate Accounting.

In the studies, subjects were exposed to a new task in the afternoon and then had a good night's sleep. These people were able to remember the task with a higher degree of efficiency than those subjects who had four hours or less of sleep. So if memory is one of the first markers of sleep deprivation, and you're supposed to be in school to remember a bunch of stuff from those classes, then maybe a little more sleep would help the whole college outcome? Just saying.

Everyone's heard of the Freshman Fifteen, but did you realize that lack of sleep could be the reason why you have to shop for new jeans at semester break? When sleep deprivation becomes normal for even a short number of days, you get hungry. Yes, the munchies set in. (I know there are *other* reasons for munchies but I'm not talking about that here. This is about sleep.) You may wander out of bed and meet up with Little Debbie® in the kitchen. Or maybe it's the food court that calls your name after class. This need to feed is a direct result of too little sleep.

When you're sleep deprived, your levels of a hormone called leptin are reduced. If you don't know leptin, let me introduce you. This spiffy little hormone is the hunger hormone. It has a few different functions. It stays on the lookout, surveying your energy balance, and then turns on your munchies or tells you to step away from the bagel. But when you aren't getting enough sleep, leptin levels drop. Signals are sent that you need more energy and your body knows that if you're not getting sleep, well, a midnight meet up with Ben and Jerry's® might do the trick.

Are you sleeping enough? Your body needs a solid 7-8 hours a day. Naps help. Everyone knows that you are not going to make it through college without mastering the art of the nap. But without those long periods of solid sleep, you will set yourself up for a trip to the health center, lapses in memory retention, and a muffin top or love handles. This is the not-so-pretty side of sleep deprivation.

## The Stupidest Thing I Ever Did Because I Was Sleep-Deprived:

*"I was trying to call my friend to relive what happened the night before but accidentally called my mom and told all the wonderful details to her."*

# Tips for Dealing with Sleep Deprivation:

## Tip #1:
Find Your Bed

It is there. Under that pile of books, dirty towels and your roommate's empty pizza box, there is a bed. Unfortunately, at school your bed gets used for a lot of things besides sleeping. Sometimes you live in your bed, watching endless Netflix®. Sometimes your bed is a food court as you lay out chips and wings for an impromptu party. And sometimes your bed becomes an elevated, bouncy dance floor for the pre-game. Whatever else happens in your bed, you also need to make sure it is available to sleep in.

Try to make sure your bed is available for sleeping. Move the stuff, wash your sheets once in a while and make a haven for some rest.

## Tip #2:
Talk to Your Roommate

At 3 AM Thursday morning you hear the familiar late-night garble and banging. You're snuggled comfy in your bed and your roommate stumbles in, waking you by tripping over the trash can. Maybe like Rebecca, the storm that is your roommate proceeds to throw up in her bed. No one wants to wake up to this. The sound of puke is not conducive to sleep. My own roommate freshman year slept on the top bunk above me and once showered my bed with puke in the middle of the night. The stories of late night roommate catastrophes are wide and varied. The unwelcome guest, the hometown high school girlfriend or the one night no-name hook-up, are reasons not to sleep in your bed. And the anxiety-ridden, Adderall®-popping roomie who never turns out the light before 4 AM is yet another. Roommates and all their idiosyncrasies will keep you from sleeping.

Have a talk. Your RA Freshman year told you this. Your parents told you this.  You know this. It is your room, too. If your roommate is keeping you from getting your sleep, it is time to talk. Don't piss them off by making accusations, because there may be some night when you aren't that well behaved and you wake them up by throwing cheese popcorn at their head. But set some ground rules for noise, guests and late-night behavior. If late-night studying must be done, have an agreement to do it outside the room. If guests are going to stay over, have a policy for giving advance notice. And talk about getting ready in the morning without setting an obnoxiously loud alarm or slamming drawers. Julia's roommate had an annoying habit of lighting a candle every morning when she put on her make up. The smell of the match burning and the honeysuckle-scented candle woke Julia up at 8 am and she didn't have class until 11:00. Be considerate. Be open. And most importantly, take the time to have the conversation.

## Tip #3:
Stop Stressing (Right...)

Two papers are due, your work schedule just got posted, and the guy you were going to ask to your date party has stopped texting. You might be able to get the papers done if you stay up for the next two nights. You might need to blow off work. You might not have a date to this weekend's party. You are officially stressed.

Everyone is stressed. That's how we roll. That's how we get stuff done. But stress also keeps us awake. Say you get the papers done, a friend can switch work schedules with you, and the dream guy starts texting. Your stress is lower...for now. But living with a lot of stress can keep you from getting a good night's sleep, even when it has passed.

A hormone called cortisol is produced when we're stressed. This hormone also mobilizes stored sugar for energy and it keeps us awake and alert. Adrenaline is the other stress hormone that most of us know about. One of the big differences between these two major stress hormones is the length of time they stay active. Adrenaline is the hormone that allows you to run from your apartment to the print store to class and get the paper turned in on time. Unfortunately, these superhuman properties quickly fade when the stressful situation subsides. But cortisol sticks around. Kind of like a watchdog. Your body just wants to make sure it's alert in case the bear that chased you down the street circles back around. Cortisol levels can stay elevated for several days after the stressful event. You just never know what's around the corner.

## The Stupidest Thing I Ever Did Because I Was Sleep-Deprived:

*"I was coming back from my 8 AM class freshman year. I lived in the back corner room on the third floor, but I was so exhausted, I only went to the second floor, walked all the way to what I thought was my room, put my key in the door and couldn't figure out why it wouldn't turn. Then some girl answered the door and asked if I was okay. That's finally when I realized I was on the wrong floor..."*

When these hormone levels are high, the other hormones that make you go to sleep don't take action. You lie awake thinking about more stressful situations. So you gotta de-stress to get good sleep.

Go to that yoga class, walk slowly through the quad, call a friend to grab a bite, sit somewhere by yourself and breathe. These are good times right now. Don't let stress ruin the fun, make you sick and keep you up at night.

## Tip #4:
Make a Date with Sleep

You have to go to class. You or your parents or your scholarship is paying a lot of money for you to be successful at school. You have to do your schoolwork and maybe work a job or play a sport. Those are the mandatory aspects of college life. And, you want to have fun. This is the time of your life when you get to have fun. Almost no questions asked. (Your roommates may inquire as to why you slept on the floor last night, but otherwise most people know and understand college is about fun.) But, in order to be successful at all of those things, you must sleep. In order to sleep, you're going to have to make it a priority. You are going to consciously have to schedule your sleep.

Do you keep it in your phone? Campus planner? Written on your arm? We all keep our schedule or appointments and assignments recorded somewhere. In order to get enough sleep you may just need to think of it as an important meeting with a person who is going to give you a killer summer internship. Would you miss that appointment? Of course not. So don't miss your sleep.

Look at your day and actually think to yourself, "I think I will try to be in bed by 11:00 tonight." Early bedtime doesn't work for you? Then pick the day that you can sleep in and do it. It's time to act like sleep is an important part of your day and not an event that takes place only when you're so exhausted that you fall asleep at your desk. Go to bed.

# Stupid Stopped

The sound of gravel and scraping jolted Dom awake. His instincts kicked in as he grabbed the steering wheel and quickly turned the car back into his lane. On his way home from school after finals he'd fallen asleep at the wheel. He'd veered onto the shoulder and when his head popped up, the guardrail was right in front of him! (This is the freaking scariest thing ever. I hope it hasn't happened to you.)

Dom called his parents and told them he'd be late arriving back home. He got off at the next exit and headed to a McDonald's parking lot, pulled into a spot in the back of the lot and slept for an hour. Dom averted stupid for the rest of his trip home. Driving while sleep-deprived is stupid. Take the time for a nap.

# Chapter 3

# **Over-Caffeinated**

## Have you ever felt over-caffeinated?

*"So one time I drank like 4 cups of coffee
(dumbest thing ever) and literally had word
vomit for the rest of the day."*

## Our Legal Addiction

I cut through the service road between the main library and the education building. I had to leave five minutes early for class, but it was a necessity. Just beyond this shortcut lay the machine that would jump-start my day. I slid through the side door and rubbed the quarters in my pocket together. I had a stash of change and dollar bills just for this purpose. I slipped down the corridor that faced the side door and there stood my mecca. The Pepsi® machine. I slid my money in and instant gratification and energy were mine.

Throughout my college years I had a little habit that nice healthy girls don't talk about...I drank diet soda. That bubbly, chemical-filled beverage helped me get through not just my morning, but my whole day. I had a three-a-day habit. I planned my day around my sodas. Instant energy with the pop of a lid. What's better than that?

Mine was soda, maybe yours is an energy drink, a latte, a chai tea...whatever your form, caffeine is our favorite legal stimulant. And many of us develop that habit in college when sleep is secondary to studying and partying. But is it bad? Should you stop taking something that makes you feel awake? These are the questions I asked myself about my diet soda habit. And my guess is, many of you with a caffeine habit feel the same way. And why stop? What could be wrong with it? Caffeine is natural, right?

What is caffeine, and why are we so addicted? And ultimately, should we care?

Ninety percent of Americans use caffeine. Funny, that is the same percentage of people who lack proper daily nutrients. We don't know how to get our vitamins and minerals but we sure know how to line up at Dunkin Donuts® and Starbucks® for a shot of instant energy. But is it energy? And if it does give us energy, what is the point of eating leafy greens?

---

## Have you ever felt over-caffeinated?

*"One time I drank coffee to study for a test and ended up being so jittery that I couldn't sit still and wasn't able to fall asleep until 4 AM."*

---

## Caffeine Is a Con Artist

I am highly intrigued by the world of forgery. Art forgery is my favorite genre of deception. Over the course of history, great artists have been mimicked for profit. One of the reasons there were so many

Rembrandt paintings in the past - over 1,000 of them at one point - is that every painting that looked ever so slightly like a Rembrandt would be signed by forgers.

Now there are only about 250 verified as signed, authentic Rembrandts. With the onslaught of forensic methods, a forger is easily foiled by infrared technologies and x-ray photography.

Our bodies are also infiltrated by forgers. And it is up to our brain to figure out the deception. Caffeine is the great con artist of energy.

In order to understand what caffeine is forging we must understand how energy is actually created, and the role your brain plays. Hold on. Here comes your human physiology lesson.

When a cell breaks down food, the end product is called ATP or Adenosine Triphosphate. **ATP is the energy currency for life**. It is stored in every cell. ATP is a big deal. It is synthesized in the mitochondria of the cell. We get energy from ATP when one or more of its triphosphates break away from the adenosine. When all the phosphates are broken from the adenosine, then it's time for your body to take a break. You have no more usable energy. You are now out of steam, your head is slumping ever closer to your desk. And your adenosine is looking for a place to recover. Adenosine heads to receptors in the brain, which then send a signal, "Hey, you're tired. Take a nap."

As your head is about to touch down, you suddenly remember the wonders of caffeine. And thus the greatest forgery of the century begins. **Caffeine's structure mimics adenosine.** It signs its signature and hops right into those brain receptors, tricking your brain and you into a false sense of energy. And caffeine is such a good forger, it can take your brain four to six hours to figure out you have no real ATP in your cells. This is a sham that we have embraced with great enthusiasm. And museum directors are not around to authenticate our choices.

I know I still haven't told you if caffeine is bad! It is a natural compound found in natural products. Look at coffee. It is a bean. Coffee has over 1000 different plant-based chemicals that are being studied for their effects on everything from Alzheimer's to weight loss. You can't get much more natural than a bean, or tea leaves, or cocoa pods. They all have caffeine. So no, **caffeine is not inherently bad**. But I don't think you are sucking on cocoa pods. The problem with caffeine is the form in which we take it.

If we all drank unsweetened Yerba Mate® tea, a tea made from the bark of a tree that is high in caffeine, I may not even be talking about the ill effects of caffeine.

**48**

But we have Five Hour Energy® drinks and people dying from caffeine overdoses, so we have to address the hazards of caffeine.

## Have you ever felt over-caffeinated?

*"When my housemate is over-caffeinated she gets really open with me and talks a mile a minute as she hops from story to story and back again with no warning. And when I ask her if she's had coffee, she is surprised I know every time."*

# Tips For Dealing With Caffeine

## Tip #1:
Acknowledge Your Addiction

Are you an addict? Most caffeine consumers love talking about their addiction. Unlike street drugs, you can easily joke about your refrigerator being full of nothing but Monster Energy®. Caffeine consumers generally believe the day does not start until the caffeine is consumed. Is that you? Are you ever able to get through a day without caffeine? If you stopped drinking your beverage of choice would you feel crappy? Get headaches? Lose your ability to function? You may have a caffeine addiction. Acknowledge it. It's okay. Once you know you need it, you can start being smart about how you use it.

## Tip #2:
Your Delivery System

The catalyst by which the caffeine is delivered is as important as the caffeine. Let me explain a poor delivery system. While visiting a college campus I was at a bar watching a concoction being made. Dubbed "The

Trashcan," four or five bottles of different liquors were dumped upside down into a large plastic cup. The bartender seemed to count to three and then topped the concoction off with a squirt from the soda hose, possibly Mountain Dew® or Sprite®. The final crescendo came with a can of Red Bull energy drink dumped upside down into the whole thing. This is not the most healthful way to get your caffeine.

Being aware of what else is going in your cup is the difference between an okay caffeine addiction and something that is a nightmare for your body. In the next chapter I will address sugar, fake food, chemicals and additives. But suffice it to say, caffeine, like anything else, is best in the form closest to nature. Hazelnut latte non-dairy, non-fat, fake sugar creamer is not too close to nature.

So, what's the best form of caffeine? Coffee, plain. Tea, plain. Chocolate, plain. See a pattern? All the added stuff is crap. Sugar, artificial sweeteners, artificial creamers, artificial colors – all can have a detrimental effect on your body. Your body has to work hard to detox and process this stuff, causing you to use up more energy. Crap doesn't fuel a body. Take your caffeine as simple as possible.

## Tip #3:
### Size Does Matter

Who determined that monster, mega, and super-sized amounts would be the way we should consume caffeine?

Caffeine overdose is real. And college students do it all the time. Reports of over-caffeinated students from health centers and hospitals have increased significantly over the past ten years as the amount of caffeine consumed has grown. Jitters, sweating, heart palpitations, increased heart rate, nausea, and dizziness are all symptoms of a caffeine overdose.

---

### Have you ever felt over-caffeinated?

*"I'm already hyper enough, but one day I drank a venti Chai Tea Latte, which are surprisingly highly caffeinated, and started laughing uncontrollably in the middle of class. The worst part was my teacher was probably the sexiest professor on campus and thought I was crazy. I totally lost my chance of being able to date him."*

---

None of these are fun. Everyone reacts differently to caffeine. If you're not a caffeine drinker and you decide to be a user to get through a big study night, go slow. It takes your body a while to process the caffeine and you could be overdoing it before you realize it.

Curious about how much is too much? Go to Caffeine Informer (www.CaffeineInformer.com). They have an app called, "Death by Caffeine." You can enter in your drink of choice and your weight. If I chose to drink Monster Energy Drinks I would have to drink 42 to die. Yes, that is a lot. No, I don't plan on even trying two drinks. Why? Because the negative effects of the caffeine start way before I would get to 42! Think about size. With caffeine, it *does* matter.

# Stupid Stopped

It was pledge week and Joe knew sleep would not be happening. In fact, part of what he would experience was planned exhaustion by his new brothers. The rituals vary by fraternity and organization, but suffice it to say, many a college student has been initiated into the practice of sleepless service. As the other pledges met for morning exercises at 5:00 AM, large cans of mega-powerful, caffeine-filled drinks were hitting the lips of all those guys who had only just had their heads hit the pillow a few hours ago. Joe joined in.

First mega-drink downed, he started to feel the haze of exhaustion lift. The second round of drinks were being passed around as the pledges started to circle in for their hellish routine of push-ups, crunches and a morning run. Joe passed on more caffeine. The day before had taught him something.

After pounding two of those drinks he had a not-too-welcome morning puke. That much caffeine on an empty stomach, accompanied by dehydration, had his body rebelling. Instead, he reached for a water bottle and hit the deck for the push-up challenge. Getting sick on caffeine is stupid. Joe's body didn't retaliate that morning.

# Chapter 4

# **Living on Pizza**

## **Describe How You Eat At School:**

*"One time a drunk boy on my floor ordered
2 large pizzas and ate them by himself."*

# Three a Day

Maybe it's pizza. Could be subs. Mine was bagels. The first day I set foot on my college campus as a prospective student, I learned the power of easy food. I was visiting campus as an accepted student. Mom and Dad were safely four hours away at home. I was staying with friends who so graciously introduced me to The Bagel Deli Shop. It was a tiny hole of a place. No seating. Graffiti type advertisements on the walls and hand drawn signs with cartoon-like pictures that announced the menu. Crunch n' Munch, a concoction of Turkey, Smoked Cheddar, Honey Mustard and Nacho Cheese Doritos, is one of the most popular items. Pig in Mud has ham, bacon and Swiss on a pumpernickel bagel. But for me, the smell of a steaming roast beef bagel lured me in. Roast beef, cream cheese, and spicy mustard steamed on a pumpernickel bagel. The steaming was the key. The first bite had me. It was amazing. That was around 2:00 PM. As my friends continued to show me around the uptown area, other delights like pizza by the slice, Cincinnati-style chili and ice cream were all available, and at all hours.

We headed back to my friend's dorm room to get ready for the night out. By the time we walked back uptown to the array of food choices, all I could think about was the bagel. Walking through the door of the shop, I didn't have to stop and consult the menu. I had my second roast beef bagel around 7:00 PM. Ahh. Just as good as the first time. Warm, meaty and satisfying after the beers I had in the dorm room.

After hitting a few house parties, we laughed our way all the way back uptown. It was just after midnight and the bars and restaurants were in full swing. We were hungry again. I only wanted to stop in one spot: The Bagel Deli Shop. Yes, I did it. I had a third roast beef, cream cheese and spicy mustard bagel in one day. I was setting up a bad precedent for my college diet.

## Can I Have Some M&M's® with That?

College students generally eat poorly. It is a fact. Chalk it up to being away from parents who for the last 18 years have harped on you to "eat this, it's good for you" and the plethora of readily available cheesy, fried and melted options. College life is the perfect storm of events to have you chowing down crap. I had a friend who kept a five-pound bag of M&M's on her desk. It seemed like every time she ate something she topped it off with a handful of M&M's. Her butt eventually began to show the effects of her chocolate-covered habit!

Stress eating, homesick eating, break-up eating and drunk eating all add to the already bad habits that most students develop. And yes, not everyone is happy with campus food. I had a sorority sister who hated everything in the dining hall. She used to grab the hard-boiled eggs off the salad bar, mix in some mayo and mustard and eat her egg salad concoction on saltines. Every day. Ugh.

## Describe How You Eat At School:

*"I am normally a very healthy eater but after drinking my healthy habits are really put to the test... One time my friend and I were walking home from a party and decided to order a pizza for the two of us.*

*As we proceeded to walk home we passed the "red food truck" that you can order food from late at night. We decided to get some sandwiches for an appetizer to our pizza... We also succeeded in polishing off the pizza once it arrived."*

So you eat crap. What's the big deal? Most of you worry about weight. Yes, we all know about the "Freshman Fifteen." Every school has a program that tells you not to over eat that includes tips and lessons. You know this stuff. What you may not know is why it even matters. Heck, if this isn't the time in life to indulge, when is?

## Human Physiology 101

Did you sign up for the course? If you don't understand this subject you may be turning into a middle aged, over-weight, lethargic person at the cellular level before you know it. So here are some Spark Notes® on Human Physiology.

Eating isn't about feeding your buzz, heartbreak or stress. Food is about feeding cells. Every one of your 75 trillion cells produces energy in a cycle known at the Krebs cycle. Every day, your cells convert food into energy. The mitochondria in your cells are the organisms that convert the food into ATP, the usable form. Remember back in the chapter on caffeine? Caffeine mimics this ATP. If your cells are functioning at peak performance levels, you produce energy efficiently.

Energy. Energy in the cells powers your organs. If you go for years without getting the right foods, your organs stop working efficiently. When your organs stop working well, you age. Why do you think your roommate's mom is a MILF and another forty-five year old woman is the poster child for KFC®? My guess: a lot of it comes down to how well they treated their cells over the years, starting back in college. Eating well is respecting your cells. (And your future self.) Let's visit the Emergency Room to learn more.

Have you been to the ER? (Hopefully not to have your stomach pumped!) If you haven't been, maybe you've watched "ER®." Okay, so you know what happens in the ER, right? People who are hurt get help. But say a gunshot victim is wheeled through the door at the same time as a kid with a cut. Who gets all the attention? The heroin dealer with the lug in his chest gets in. And the kid with the cut sits and waits and waits and waits. He isn't really an emergency, right? He's not going to die because he cut his finger carving a pumpkin. Heroin dealer with the gunshot wound wins every time in the emergency room. This practice of prioritizing critical care is known as triage.

Your body puts this concept into practice too. It is called **triage nutrition**. If you don't get enough nutrients to feed your cells, the critical organs get all the attention. Let's say the only vegetables in your day are the peppers and onions in your Chipotle burrito. And the next day you have leftover pizza. Somebody once told you that pizza has all the food groups so there must be a vegetable there, too. But if you are honest with yourself, you probably aren't getting five servings of fruits and vegetables every day. (And by the way, to prevent disease and aging, the number is more like 8-10 servings!) So you don't get enough nutrients from your food, so what? Life is fun! But your brain doesn't have the same laid-back attitude. Your brain is playing triage nurse!

You didn't get enough vitamins and minerals for your heart, lungs, pancreas and bones. Your brain can only wheel so many emergencies through the double doors. Your brain has to decide where the nutrients go so you can stay alive. And just like our drug dealer and pumpkin carver, the heart wins over bones every time. You aren't going to die if your bones don't get nutrients. Welcome to your aging process! Yes, you. Full-of-life pizza-eater, you are aging if you aren't eating well. And worse, you are also setting yourself up for disease!

So you need to eat better. You need to eat real, whole foods, stuff that grew on a tree or came from the ground, in order to feed your cells, so they make energy, so your organs work, so you don't get sick and start to look like your Uncle Frank. Eating well is about more than flabby abs and a big butt. Eating well is about you feeling good, aging well and keeping disease away.

## Sugar on Top

But you like late night cookies. And pizza. And beer. College students are carb eaters. Cheese Fries 101 is a prerequisite for any major. Sharing a tube of cookie dough with your roommate is a rite of passage. And anything on a white bun on a Saturday morning after drinking is a superfood. But all that sugar in the form of carbs or straight up sugar is damaging your cells, making you tired and chunkifying your butt.

Before we talk about what sugar does, let's clarify what it is. Yes it is the white stuff, but it's so much more. Besides the more than fifty different names of sugar, which include evaporated beet juice, cane juice crystals and high fructose corn syrup, any carbohydrate that has been stripped of its nutrients is also sugar. Buns at White Castle®, mac n' cheese at Noodle and Company®, and cookies at Insomnia Cookies® are all sugar. White flour and beer break down into sugar. So if you're thinking you're a not a candy bar kind of person, if you're a carb eater, you're getting sugar.

Besides making you gain weight, sugar has other evil practices. Yes, I did say evil. Pretend I'm your cells talking. Sugar is a serial killer, an animal abuser, a Snapchat screen-shot taker. Bad stuff. Sugar affects your cells in three evil ways.

## Describe How You Eat At School:

*"I like to say that the 'Freshman 15' is not gained by drinking, but rather drunk eating... how can you resist when every time you are walking home there are people selling pizza, cookies, or fresh pancakes to fundraise for a good cause?!"*

First, it makes your body work too hard. Sugar has to be pushed into either your cells or you liver. And this has to happen fast. Sugar can't just aimlessly float around your body like that lame guy who hovers around the bars at 2 AM waiting for drunk girls. It has to get in bed with your cells quick. And in order to do this, your pancreas has to make insulin. Insulin is the wingman. But if you abuse your wingman, he's going to leave you. And that is what happens with insulin. You abuse your body by eating too much sugar, and over time your pancreas and insulin feel abused. They can't keep up with your sugar-swilling shenanigans and they bug out. You end up with diabetes. It can be a slow process, taking years to get you to this point. But if you don't get sugar consumption under control, your body will wear out. You will get a disease.

Second, sugar is a digestive bully. I know you've heard of bullying. Yep, every school, team and organization has told you about bullying. And although deliberately hurting someone through relentless taunting is horrible, the type of bodily bullying I'm talking about can make you feel physically miserable for life. When your body starts digesting food, sugar yells out, "Me first!" So you've chowed down on three pieces of pizza and then topped it off with a Frappuccino. That frozen coffee delight has 54 grams of sugar in it, or the equivalent of two Hershey Bars®. Your stomach makes a bunch of enzymes to digest all that food. But as soon as the sugar hits your stomach, digesting the pizza stops. Sugar is the bully and wants to be first. All this stopping and starting of digestion leads to a bunch of bad digestive mojo. Heartburn, stomachache, diarrhea, constipation, gas. But that is only the beginning. While you're feeling bad, your digestive tract is being damaged. Keep this up and you'll be unable to properly digest, absorb and use your food to power your life. Diseases of the digestive tract are not sexy.

And finally, sugar pushes good stuff out of the cells. A battle happens at the cellular level when sugar enters the cells. You have to battle germs, viruses and bacteria every day. Just walking into the shower of your dorm, brushing your teeth in a communal sink and sitting next to someone hacking through class could set you up for a weekend spent in bed. Especially if you have a sugar habit. When levels of sugar in the cell are high, immune response is low.

White blood cells act as your body's defenders. In order keep you out of the health center, white blood cells partner up with a big dose of Vitamin C. But sugar has a similar chemical structure as Vitamin C. Those darn white blood cells take sugar into the cell instead of C. The white blood cell gets overloaded with sugar and never takes in the Vitamin C. If blood sugar rises to levels of only 120... which can be obtained with a soda and a couple cookies...the white blood cell's ability to absorb and destroy bacteria is reduced by 75%! It can take white blood cells four to six hours to return to active duty! And soon you're in bed with the chills and missing your mommy.

Sugar and simple carbs that convert to sugar are not the foods that are going to help you through the grueling task of being a student. You will set yourself up for disease, get fat, get sick and generally not feel good when you overindulge in sugar.

## The Gum Isn't Blue

When my daughter went to Spain on a student trip, we had very little communication back and forth. But one day she was able to send me a quick Facebook® message from an Internet café. I asked her about the food. Her response, which I totally understood, was, "The gum isn't blue." I'd been harping on my kids for years that we didn't need bright orange mac n' cheese, green sports drinks or blue gum. Artificial colors, preservatives, and chemical flavorings are all stuff you may be putting in your body that make you feel like crap. Fake food is not what your cells want.

When chemicals clog your system, all the organs that keep your body clean work harder. Your liver is the key player here. Remember in Chapter 1 we talked about respecting your liver? Well that bag of Doritos® is a direct insult. Your liver has to work again.

Really, if you think you're working hard to make it through school...think about your liver. It detoxifies and cleanses your body by continuously filtering the blood of poisons that enter it through the digestive tract, the skin, and the respiratory system. So, it only makes sense that if your liver is working overtime to detox the chemicals you just threw in from your Pringles®, Diet Coke®, and Skittles®, you're going to get tired. Your body works. Your organs do their jobs. But just like you, when you start piling on the exams, deadlines, extreme workouts, stress; you feel overloaded.

And when your liver becomes overworked by all the chemicals you're eating, your entire system can be thrown off balance, and your health severely compromised. Too much fake food is a stupid choice.

## Describe How You Eat At School:

*"Every day I think 'I'll eat better tomorrow' but then never do. I have a lot of self-confidence, so being a little curvier doesn't bother me but I'm very unhealthy. The microwave is my best friend."*

# Tips for Eating

## Tip #1:
Find Fruits and Vegetables

Yes, they are there. In every dining hall, in the mini marts, and off-campus dining options, fruits and vegetables do exist. Eat them. Stop shunning them, thinking, "Oh my mom made me eat those at home. I'm not going to eat them here. I'm all good with fries." If your decision is to go without, it is your loss. So how do you do it? Look. Open your eyes and commit to a vegetable at lunch and dinner. Fruit isn't so hard to fit in but vegetables you have to decide to friend. No one else but you can pick up the carrot sticks, make the salad, ask for the veggie stir-fry. You must make this part of your food plan.

## Tip #2:
Can I Get a Take Out Menu?

You know you will order out. How can you make this a better process for your health? Sit down for a minute. Get your top five favorite take out menus. (Maybe you have ten!) Actually take the time to look at them. Have you studied the menu at Jimmy Johns®? Did you know that most sub places have more than lettuce to add to a sandwich? You can add cucumbers at Jimmy Johns. Cucumbers help detox your liver! Add mushrooms or spinach to pizza. Choose vegetable spring rolls instead of pork egg rolls. Change your menu mindset.

## Tip #3:
### Why Is There a Pizza In My Bed?

Food shows up in your room like jocks at the gym. It is inevitable. But just because you can eat in your room doesn't mean you should. I know Mom sends packages or your roommate has a snack basket or your suitemate buys food for everyone so she doesn't have to eat alone. Yes, food shows up. But try to keep "room food" to a minimum. If you reduce the food eaten in your room, you will reduce the number of bad snacks and amount of take out food.

## Tip #4:
### Food Emergencies

Plan for the emergency. It will come. You're studying. You can't make it one more minute. You must eat. Make a list of your favorite real whole snack foods. Items that would not turn up on this list are: Slim Jims and Pringles. If you don't remember what these real foods are, they grew on a tree or in the ground. When you go to the grocery store for some supplies, get nuts, power bars with less than 10 grams of sugar, fruit, individual hummus cups, almond butter and pita. Have some "go to" snacks that you can keep in your backpack or room so your first call in a food emergency is not pizza delivery.

---

## Describe How You Eat At School:

*"I eat everything in sight, literally. I can only keep healthy things in my dorm because I would gain 395482390482309482 more pounds than I already have."*

---

## Tip #5:
I'll Second That Emotion

Seventy-five percent of all eating in this country is emotional. We eat when we're stressed, angry, and frustrated. Those are head emotions and usually require something crunchy or chewy. We relieve stress by chomping on chips, pizza crusts and cookies. When we're lonely, depressed, or unfulfilled, we meet up with our comfort food friends like Ben and Jerry. We use food to make us feel good. But after the dopamine receptors in your brain get the pleasure hit from the food, you then feel bad from your crappy food choice.

If you're an emotional eater, it's time to connect with that emotion. Every time food goes into your mouth when you aren't truly hungry, ask yourself why. If over and over you stuff Oreos® in your mouth late at night while studying, ask yourself the question, "Why do I need this cookie?" Chances are you're frustrated with your Econ paper. If you order pizza with friends when you just ate a sub a couple hours ago, assess your need.

Were you really just feeling lonely and needed company of friends? Step away from emotional eating. Start asking yourself the question: "Why am I eating this?"

# Stupid Stopped

Freshman year Rebecca kept a pink plastic bin sitting on top of her dorm fridge. When her parents dropped her off at school, her mother filled it to the top with a food warehouse-sized package of bags of chips and Cheetos®. Rebecca grew to crave the basket of crap. Whenever she got a package from home, she refilled the basket with candy bars and chips. If she ever caught a ride to Wal-Mart®, she bought more individual-sized snacks. The basket became her habit. Leave the room; grab a snack. Come into the room; grab a snack. Study break; grab a snack. And by Thanksgiving, as every college wellness center forewarns, she was on her way to the Freshman 15. Rebecca had never had her pants feel so tight. Yoga pants became her new wardrobe go-to. She was feeling a bit bad about her weight gain, but eating made her feel good.

When spring rolled around, and shorts and flip-flops returned to campus, Rebecca finally took a hard look at the habit she had developed. Why did she need the basket of crap? She got smart enough to ask herself the hard question. It had become an emotional crutch to her. At home she walked through the door and was greeted by her brothers or parents. Someone was there.

But walking into an empty dorm room wasn't fun. She fueled her lonely times with food.

But, wanting to get back into her summer wardrobe, Rebecca dumped the basket of crap, and filled it with her shorts and bikinis. Her roommate thought she was going out of town, but Rebecca had finally stopped being stupid about emotional eating. She used her basket instead to remind her that the emotional eating had to stop if she wanted to feel good about herself.

Don't be stupid; ask yourself the hard questions about what you're eating.

## Describe How You Eat At School:

*"My freshman year I would go at about 9 PM to the market and buy a ton of unhealthy snacks. Pizza, cookies, ice cream (lots of it), and candy. I felt so gross afterwards. One time after working out, my roommate and I ordered a pizza and wings."*

# Are You Done With Stupid?

You made it! Or maybe you just read the quotes of other students. Either way, I hope I got you thinking about the lifestyle you're choosing. You're going to make some decisions that compromise your health while you're in college. But don't be stupid about your health.

How you treat your body today sets you up for the rest of your life. You really don't want to look like that lady in the neighborhood who scares all the little kids. And you really don't want to deal with disease.

Take a few steps today to take care of you. Small changes work. Go to my website, www.KathyParry.com, and download the **FREE Resource: Students Stopping Stupid**. Please contact me with your success stories at Kathy@KathyParry.com, or post them on my Facebook page.

And I'd love to meet you! Contact your school to bring me to speak! I can speak at student activities events, Panhellenic and IFC retreats, Parent's Weekends, and Student Orientations. Learn more at www.KathyParry.com.

Wishing you a smart life!

Kathy                                    *Keep reading →*

P.S. As a **special bonus**, I've included one more chapter with tips on staying out of the Health Center! If you're not adopting some of these practices in your life... you will end up in the creepy halls of the Health Center!

P.P.S. And are you ready for one more **FREE Bonus**? Go to www.KathyParry.com for your **FREE Guide to a More Energetic Life**.

Bonus Chapter

# Stay Away From the Health Center

## Call the Health Center

Six weeks. That is the mark. By about the middle of October campus health centers fill up with cases of inflamed tonsils, infected sinuses, and intestinal cruds. The student body is sick. It takes about six weeks of being hung over, over-caffeinated, sleep-deprived and living on pizza to run your immune function into the ground.

You will wake up one morning, or attempt to wake up, and realize you feel like crap. Your mom is nowhere to be found. But you call her anyway. She can't take your temperature, she can't do the mom diagnosis thing, and she can't call the doctor. You earned this cold, flu, or infection. You have to deal with it now. You stick your ear buds in, grab a few rough sheets of toilet paper to blow your nose, and stumble your way out the door. Off to the health center you go.

But wouldn't it be so much better if you didn't have to sit in the stale waiting room of the health center with all the other miserable, nose-running, fever-filled students? If you begin to follow a few of the tips in this book, you will greatly increase the chances of keeping your immune function strong. Disrespecting your immune function is a stupid idea. So show your cells some love and help keep bacteria, viruses and infections away.

# Tips for Avoiding the Health Center

## Tip #1:

Love Your Gut

Over half of your immune function happens in your gut. That's all the stuff that happens below your stomach. So think of small intestines, large intestines and colon. Sexy stuff. Here in the mushy section of you lives a host of microbes that help you stay well.

You've probably heard about "good bacteria." If your mom had you eating yogurt she was probably all about this good stuff. But yogurt, especially if it's filled with sugar and artificial junk, doesn't do all that much for your immune function. Probiotics are the good bacteria that live in your intestinal tract. More microbes live in your gut than cells in your body! We need these beneficial bacteria to maintain our immune function and to absorb nutrients. I would tell every student going off to school to pack a good probiotic. Look for probiotics that have at least 2 billion strains, and refrigerate after opening.

Probiotics do not need to be taken on a continuous basis. Generally a course of two weeks is a good rebuilding time frame. Taking a few weeks off lets your body naturally adjust levels.

## Tip #2:
### Loving On The C

Everyone has heard of Vitamin C for a cold. Remember back in the sugar section of the last chapter where I told you that sugar pushed Vitamin C out of your cells?

Well, you may have a bunch of cells without Vitamin C, and they aren't going to do their job fighting off viruses and evil lurking germs. But swigging huge glasses of OJ in the dining hall isn't necessarily the answer.

Some juice is okay. But big old 12-ounce glasses spike your insulin and drive the sugar in the OJ into the cells, thus defeating the purpose of drinking OJ for the Vitamin C. Always best to get your Vitamin C from pieces of whole fruit. The whole piece of fruit has the fiber and all the good nutrients that get the C into the cell. Grab that orange, pineapple, bunch of grapes or even red peppers for the real C.

## Tip #3:

Drink Yourself Healthy

Guess what? That doesn't mean alcohol, lattes, or energy drinks. That is water. Yes, we're back to good old H2O. Every cell needs it for every function. And most importantly, your cells need water to support immune function.

We are a nation of chronically dehydrated people. Remember how alcohol dehydrates? As a college student you should NEVER find yourself without a water bottle.

Get in the habit of keeping one with you at all times. And my secret of the day...Stop in your favorite coffee shop...Starbucks, Caribou®, Peets®, etc. Their water is almost always highly filtered and tasty! Ask for a Grande water to go.

## Tip #4:

Wash Your Hands, Dude

I really shouldn't even have to go here. You learned this in preschool. Just do it. This is how germs are spread.

# Tip #5:
## Wash Your Towel

Okay, maybe you didn't learn this one in pre-school. But your towel holds a host of germs. Yes, a colony of gross lives in your towel. You rub skin cells off your body as you dry yourself. Cells stick to the fabric. And soon your towel is full of yummy snacks for bacteria, which thrive in damp places. When you reuse your towel, the bacteria can be transferred back to your body. A regular swap fest of germs.

Your towel should be washed at least every few days. I get it; you may not do laundry that often. At least try to go to school with a few towels. Should I even discuss your sheets? Wash those too. Really, the stuff in your bed can make you sick.

# Stupid Stopped

Nick wanted to go out. It was Thursday night and the scene would be good. But this thing was going on in the back of his throat. He knew the tickle he felt might be nothing, or it could be the beginnings of something. His suite-mates were already pre-partying in the room down the hall. He stared at his Organic Chemistry book and felt exhausted.

"You coming, Nick?" he heard from down the hall.

"Yeah...I'm coming," he called back.

Nick felt a cough forming in the back of his throat. He hacked a few times and looked at his book again. Midterms were two weeks away and he was borderline. All he really wanted to do was get some sleep.

A friend poked his head in Nick's room. "You ready?"

"Hey, I think I'm passing. I'm not feeling great," replied Nick.

"Pussy," he said as he left the room.

Nick ran down to mini-mart in the next dorm over. He was pretty sure he'd find something that might taste good. He grabbed an apple and an orange and a bottle of water. He finished his chapter in Chem and turned out his light. He barely heard his friends come in later. And as he crossed campus the next morning on his way to class, he had a sense that his choice the night before may have helped him divert a trip to the health center.

# About Kathy Parry

Kathy Parry is passionate about food - real food. She helps others understand what real, whole foods are and how they affect health and vitality. Raised by parents who grew a garden full of vegetables, Kathy has long embraced a whole food diet. Food has the power to transform health and Kathy wants to share her love of eating whole, real foods with you.

Kathy Parry – Your Real Food Coach
*Author, Speaker, Mother of 4*

With degrees in Business and Food Management, Kathy set out to change the world of food; but first she trained bankers. Feeling pressured, she gave in to the idea that "all serious people go into banking," where Kathy discovered her love for standing up in front of people as she developed and delivered training programs for a super-regional bank in the South. After leaving the world of banking, Kathy jumped at the chance to get back to her real passion and she began to sell imported and specialty foods. This immersion into food fueled her desire to encourage others to eat real food. Soon, those others she was encouraging came in the form of four children.

Pureeing organic broccoli and avoiding Happy Meals became the food activities that filled her days. But it was child number four that changed the way Kathy viewed food. After a tumultuous six months of not knowing why her child who had daily, uncontrollable seizures was not thriving, Kathy finally got answers.

Merritt Joy was diagnosed with a mitochondrial disease. Her cells didn't metabolize food properly. Kathy spent the next several years becoming an expert in cellular function and received her certification in plant-based nutrition from T. Colin Campbell Program at eCornell University. Now twelve years later, Merritt Joy has never been hospitalized or suffered from any of the debilitating viruses the doctors feared. She is highly disabled, but very healthy.

While Merritt's condition could have been the flat tire that ruined Kathy's food journey, it instead became the impetus for the passion that takes her and others to places of great health and vitality.

*Kathy Parry – Your Real Food Coach™* is Kathy's speaking and coaching business. She helps others through corporate wellness programs, event and keynote speaking and college and association programming. To learn more about how Kathy can inspire your group to live an energetic life, read the next page for details.

## Connect with Kathy Parry On Social Media to Receive More Tasty Tips:

 www.KathyParry.com/facebook

 www.KathyParry.com/pinterest

 www.KathyParry.com/twitter

# Stop Stupid On Your Campus!

<u>Your Campus Needs Speakers</u>! **Student Orientation, Parents Weekends, Panhellenic and IFC Events, Health and Wellness Programming, and Office of Student Activities...all need to schedule dynamic speakers!**

Give me a call! My events are full of energy, humor and inspiration. Let me work with your group to help stop the stupid!

Choosing a speaker is an important decision. Your audience will thank you for choosing a professional, fun, entertaining speaker! To request your speaking

Kathy During a Keynote Presentation with Eye Opening Demonstrations!

brochure today and sign up for a FREE Report: "Ten Ways to Stay Energized" at www.KathyParry.com.

## Five Reasons Meeting, Event and College Campuses Love Booking Kathy Parry:

**1. Experienced Speaker:** Kathy has given hundreds of lectures, workshops and seminars to groups, clubs, associations and businesses.

**2. Fascinating Facts:** By keeping up to date on the most current food and health related topics, Kathy keeps audiences enthralled with information.

**3. Fun and Humorous:** As a mother of four, Kathy is relaxed and shares the humorous stories from her family's front lines. She is spontaneous and feeds off the audience to keep everyone engaged.

**4. Real and Authentic:** You'll hear the good and the bad habits that Kathy has experienced on her own journey to wellness. (Yes, she used to drink Diet Pepsi!)

**5. A Powerful Coach:** Kathy uses coaching techniques to inspire her audiences to make immediate changes.

---

## To schedule Kathy for your next event:

Call 412-427-1137 or Email Kathy@KathyParry.com

# Want to learn even more about feeling your best?

Order Kathy's other book at
www.KathyParry.com!

Do you need caffeine and chocolate to make it through your day? Are you dragging by mid-afternoon? Unfocused? Unproductive?

You're not alone. Millions of people feel tired and sluggish – even worn down – on a daily basis.

The Ultimate Recipe for an Energetic Life gives you the information you need and desire to finally feel vital and productive!

Inside you will learn:

- The six simple steps you must take to live an energetic and engaged life!

- How to uncover the foods you're eating right now

that are wreaking havoc on your body and keeping you tired all day long!

- Easy, delicious, and healthful recipes that will save you time and boost your energy levels so you can not only "keep up" – you can speed up!

Each chapter teaches you important information about how you are sabotaging your energy levels, while giving you tips and tactics to combat these habits. You'll receive action steps that will give you a starting point for change. AND...each chapter includes delicious, healthful recipes designed for busy people.

**PLUS:** A FREE BONUS CHAPTER INCLUDED: "20 Super-foods for More Energy Including 5 Additional Energy Boosting Recipes!" Go to www.KathyParry.com today!

---

*"Kathy is pure radiant energy. Her daughter Merritt has long outlived medical expectations. I attribute both to the scientific yet simple recipes and knowledge behind Kathy's life work: feeding our mitochondria with clean nutritious foods that lead to positive energy and health."* Amy Goldstein MD Director, Neurogenetics & Metabolism Children's Hospital Pittsburgh

*"Kathy's passion for eating real whole food is contagious. Her ideas for gaining energy are easy to implement and the recipes are great! Her book opened my eyes to the types of foods we need to feel energetic."* James Malinchak, Featured on ABC's Hit TV Show "Secret Millionaire" and Founder, www.BigMoneySpeaker.com